Analyze Yourself-

enabling anyone to become deeply
psycho - analyzed without a personal
analyst

by

E. Pickworth Farrow
M.A., D.SC.
With Foreword by the late
Professor Sigmund Freud
M.D., LLD., FOR.MEM.R.S.

INTERNATIONAL UNIVERSITIES PRESS

New York   New York

Printing Statement:

Due to the very old age and scarcity of this book,
many of the pages may be hard to read due to the
blurring of the original text, possible missing pages,
missing text and other issues beyond our control.

Because this is such an important and rare work, we
believe it is best to reproduce this book regardless of
its original condition.

Thank you for your understanding.

Foreword

THE AUTHOR of this book is known to me as a man of strong and independent intelligence who, probably on account of a certain wilfulness of character, could not get on well with the two analysts with whom he experimented. He then had recourse to a consistent application of the process of self-analysis which I had once used myself in order to analyze my own dreams. His results deserve notice, especially because of his special individuality and his technique.

SIGMUND FREUD

Preface

THIS BOOK contains a full and detailed account of how
to follow a practical method of the psycho-analysis of
one's own mind, with some results from early childhood
obtained by pursuing it in the author's own case. Anyone should be able to follow the process, on the basis of
the instructions given, with considerable improvement
to his former state of health and happiness.

Unpleasant incidents in his life will probably come to
light, or be recollected, but it will be found that the
emotion attached to them can be removed by continuing the process by which they have been recollected.

Repressed emotion and unhappiness in the mind has
a crippling effect all through life unless it is remembered and recognized, and is thus able to be removed.
Anyone will realize this fact very clearly after such
repressed material has been removed from his own
mind and his health has greatly improved as a result.
It is the removal of repressed emotion which produces
the improvement in health that is the aim of psycho-
analytic therapy, for it must be remembered that the
object of the process is not the mere recollection of incidents *per se*—whether in the years of childhood or otherwise—although this recollection is a necessary preliminary to the removal of repressed emotion from the
recollected incidents.

Forces outside the individual have many direct and
indirect injurious effects upon him while others have ·
very beneficial effects. Analysis enables one to remove

the results of many of the injurious influences while retaining the beneficial ones. Needless to say, this is of great advantage to the individual.

The author was very critical of analysis to begin with, but experience has thoroughly convinced him of its value when properly handled. He considers that now this process and its ultimately very beneficial effects have been discovered continually improved forms of it will probably remain as therapeutic measures indefinitely—or until they are superseded by more rapid and effectual methods in their own field. Any such better methods, however, would probably need to be founded upon, or at least could not ignore, the results of analytic experience and the very important psychological discoveries and notable cures that have followed. The exact details of how the therapeutic effect of psycho-analysis arises may present big problems but the effect is certainly there and to a very marked extent. For instance, in the author's own case it has greatly increased his cheerfulness and his interest in country life; in such things as swimming, gardening and golf, and has greatly reduced any former tendency to introspection by removing its causes.

There seems little doubt that Professor Freud was the "Darwin of the Mind" even if time should eventually show that some of his views were not quite correct. By his use of the process of "free-association" he certainly opened out an entirely new field of mental investigation and therapeutics, incidentally making the very important discoveries of "resistance" and "repression" in the process. Psychology, before his day, did not make any very striking discoveries chiefly because it had no knowledge of this process of "repression". He certainly changed psychology from being what many people considered a somewhat dull and uninteresting subject into a very interesting one.

This book includes the results of more than 2,800 hours' research work spread over a period of 18 years, and the production of more than 12,000,000 words of free-association. The material produced, and given here, was examined and observed in a very critical and scientific way by the author and was repeatedly checked objectively wherever possible by questioning those adults who were associated with him in his infancy. This book is the first of an entirely new kind of auto-biography dealing with those experiences of the individual which have been repressed into the unconscious on account of their erstwhile painful nature, and which are only recoverable by the penetrating effect of psycho-analysis. It is hoped that it may be followed by a number of similar autobiographies, for the co-ordination of the material in a number of such life stories would doubtless prove of considerable scientific value.

It is hoped that the description of the method of self-analysis which this book contains may also be found useful for practical work in conjunction with the reading of other books upon analysis. Such books frequently remind the reader of incidents in his own life and childhood; and the method of self-analysis described in the present work would enable him to remove the emotion associated with these incidents and thus assist his own analysis. A number of books for further reading are mentioned at the end of this book.

The results obtained in ordinary analysis show that the central nervous system is fundamentally far more closely and compactly organized in its working than is commonly supposed, and that it is solely the presence of the complexes and repressions which prevents this fact from being generally recognized.

The analytic process gives one much interesting information concerning the extremely complicated and intertwined working of the thought processes in the adult human mind and enables one to understand his own mind, as well as those of other people, far better than before. Amongst other things the process of self-analysis, as described here, as well as ordinary analysis, shows that the so-called "herd-instinct" is capable of being split-up into various elements, and groups of elements, founded upon fears and affection—chiefly upon fears—and that it is not a separate instinct properly so-called.

Non-analytical psychology scratches about on the surface of the mind leaving all the deeper origins of the conscious thoughts and reactions permanently hidden from examination. These deeper origins are far more important causally than the specific conscious thoughts themselves.

The author considers that it is the operation of the underlying self-preservative instinct which is the fundamental cause in the production of neurosis, and that the presence of repressed sexual factors, while probably practically universal and frequently extremely important, is secondary to this underlying basis. (See Chapter 9.)

There can be no doubt that neurotic people, such as

people suffering from feelings of inferiority, are far commoner than is generally supposed. The term "inferiority feelings" is undoubtedly preferable to "inferiority complex" for the feelings referred to normally depend upon the combined effect of a number of repressed complexes in the mind. A wrinkled forehead or any kind of strain in the expression is a strong indication of the presence of one or more severe complexes of which the individual is quite unconscious. A person in good mental health has a restful face. As stated, the author found this method of self-analysis extremely beneficial to his own health after being with two professional analysts, and this would also very probably apply to other people. It is very suitable for removing inferiority feelings and other neurotic symptoms and may be specially useful in war time for relieving cases of war strain when many people may be unable to visit a personal analyst.

Analysis by a professional analyst is, in any case, too expensive for many people who would be greatly benefited by the process. Also the number of professional analysts is far too small to deal with the vast number of people whom the process would benefit. Thus this method of self-analysis will doubtless prove very useful. A further advantage is that the common, although usually unfounded, criticism that the external analyst reads the results into the mind of his patient obviously cannot apply to this method because such an external analyst is not present.

It will be noted that the process of self-analysis described consists in observational work by the individual upon the products of free-association from his own

mind—exactly the same in principle as the observational method of research employed in other branches
of biology. This observational research upon the working of his own mind has been much the most interesting
kind of scientific work that the author has yet encountered. Observation and experiment have always seemed
to him far more important than mere theory. The late
Sir J. J. Thomson said to him, a few years ago, in relation to his own electron theory, "Well, of course I've
always thought that the chief value of a theory was as a
basis for further experiments". On this extremely sound
and illuminating view, the chief value of psycho-
analytic theory also must lie in provoking experiments,
both by the analysis of individuals (and noting the
effects on their health) and in bringing up children
differently.

Professor Freud wrote that "It is quite superfluous
for any science which can offer a real contribution to
knowledge to strive to make itself heard and to win
adherents. Its reception must depend upon its results,
and it can afford to wait until these have compelled
attention". It would appear that Sir J. J. Thomson
and Professor Freud both thought that "An ounce of
practice is worth a pound of theory". Every sensible
person must naturally agree with this view.

In the author's opinion the great improvement in a
person's health and mental liveliness which is produced
by deep analysis indicates that careful and critical
psycho-analytical researches are very important from
the point of view of increasing human happiness and
mental health in the future. This is apart altogether
from their biological and general scientific interest,

which is considerable.

It may be mentioned that the author is not a practising analyst, his interest in the subject being solely one of scientific research and the improvement of his own health and that of other people.

The author's thanks are due to Mr. Harold Burbidge for help in revising the whole of the book, and to Drs. J. H. Power and J. Stanley White, and Mr. H. G. Bolam for revising various parts; also to Sir Robert Armstrong-Jones, C.B.E., M.D., and the late Sir Frederick Mott, K.B.E., M.D., F.R.S., for making useful suggestions. His old friend, Professor Tansley, has given him a great deal of help in the final preparation of this book for the Press. His thanks are also due to the Editors of the following journals in which most of the material originally appeared for permission to reprint it, viz., *Psyche*, *The British Journal of Medical Psychology*, *The International Journal of Psycho-Analysis*, *The Medical Press*, *The Journal of Mental Science*, *Die Internationale Zeitschrift für Psychoanalyse*, *The Journal of Neurology and Psychopathology*, *The Journal of Nervous and Mental Disease*, *The Psychoanalytic Review*, and *The American Journal of Psychology*. An abstract of one of the chapters also appeared in *The Lancet*. Some delay has occurred in republishing the material owing to the author's wish to review and criticize it as fully and as deeply as possible before republishing it in a collected form. Close and long continued criticism has not, however, made it necessary to make any appreciable alterations to the original material; but only certain improvements in the exposition and a number of additions amplifying many of the points.

E.P.F.

Preface to the Second Edition

THE AUTHOR was originally prejudiced against psychology in favour of things he could actually see. Experience has, however, caused him to modify his opinion.

Much work has been done with regard to the effects of the internal secretions of the ductless glands upon the body and upon the mind. Very little work indeed, however, appears to have been done upon the effects of severe physical and mental shocks upon the nervous system; and, with this, very probably upon the pituitary gland, and thus upon the whole of the endocrine system. This omission seems very regrettable and it is hoped that it will be remedied in the future.

E.P.F.

Contents

Chapter One

Origin of the Author's Interest in Psycho-Analysis

THE AUTHOR has heard it said that "People who are interested in analysis do not take any interest in the reasons why they are interested in this subject. They—some of them at any rate—take a very great interest in the causes which make other people interested in other subjects, but as to their own interest in psycho-analysis —well, they seem to take no interest whatever in the causes of this, and seem to have no ideas whatever upon this matter. Other people would not like to ask them about it because, of course, they are more polite than the psycho-analysts, and fear that the subject might be taboo. Still the above is the really interesting question in view of the fact that the average person takes no interest whatever in analysis and does not care anything about it".

It may be interesting if the author deals briefly with the origin of his interest in psycho-analysis. It will show that he has not ignored the above relevant question.

In the year 1912, when the author was at Cambridge, Mr. A. G. Tansley got a number of us interested in a little book which was then in proof and which was later destined to become very well known—viz. Bernard Hart's *The Psychology of Insanity*.[1]

---

[1] In the *Cambridge Manuals of Science and Literature* (Camb. Univ. Press). The author understands that this book is one of the two "best sellers" in the whole of the series. Apparently there must be large numbers of people who are interested in the subject of insanity.

I
B

The author read this little book with interest and was particularly interested in that portion of p. 70 of which the following is an extract:

Now Jung found that the reaction obtained varied considerably, according as the stimulus-word had or had not aroused a complex to activity. The reactions characteristic of the activity of a complex exhibited increase of the reaction-time and various peculiarities in the reaction-word. The following example, given by Jung and Peterson, illustrates some of the points in question:

Stimulus Word	Reaction Word	Reaction Time. Seconds
1. Head	Hair	1·4
2. Green	Meadow	1·6
3. *Water*	*Deep*	5·0
4. Stick	Knife	1·6
5. Long	Table	1·2
6. *Ship*	*Sink*	3·4
7. Ask	Answer	1·6
8. Wool	Knit	1·6
9. Spiteful	Friendly	1·4
10. *Lake*	*Water*	4·0
11. Sick	Well	1·8
12. Ink	Black	1·2
13. *Swim*	*Can swim*	3·8

The patient from whom this series was obtained had, during a recent attack of depression, determined to commit suicide by drowning. This complex had manifested itself in the associations which are italicized. 3, 6, 10 and 13 are instances of increased reaction-time; 13 shows also a peculiarity in the reaction-word itself.

The author has always had a very strong dislike of anything savouring of mysticism. Probably this attitude may have been partly the result of his training in observational biological work—where, of course, hard facts, and hard facts only, are what one is searching for the whole time. The author, however, does not believe that this is the origin of his attitude. He would like to think that his strong opposition to mysticism, and to everything mystical, is a natural attitude with him resulting from Anglo-Saxon level-headedness! However, be that as it may, this opposition to everything mystical had strongly prejudiced the author against all forms of mental investigation, and against psychology in general.

Here, however, in this extract from Dr. Hart's book, it seemed to the author that there were some definite observational facts which were not to the slightest extent mystical inferences, and which should be capable of being tackled or examined by the methods of observational biology. Chiefly owing to the interest aroused in him by the portion of Dr. Hart's book quoted above, the author then read Professor Freud's *Interpretation of Dreams* and *Psychopathology of Everyday Life*, which had recently been translated into English. Both of these books interested him, but admittedly not so much, at that time, as the above extract from Hart.

A number of years later the author thought that it would be an interesting experiment to get a friend to prepare and read over to him a long list of stimulus words and record his reaction-words and reaction-times to each of these stimulus words on the method originated by Wundt and Sir Francis Galton and later developed by Bleuler and Jung and their associates. The author was greatly interested and surprised to find how extensively his emotions varied immediately after the calling out of various stimulus-words, and also in the variation in the difficulty in finding and uttering a reply to different stimulus-words. His normal reaction time was 2 seconds; but, in addition to several other instances, he gave the following reaction words of psycho-analytical interest in reply to the stated stimulus words with the stated times, viz.:

Stimulus Words	Reaction Words	Reaction Times in Seconds
Bread	Hunger	3·8
Needle	Long	3·0
Threaten	Life	4·0
Salt	Good	3·8
Despise	Somebody	4·2
Ox	Horn	3·0
Pencil	Long	2·8
Narrow	Gulf	3·0

The above "association test" is certainly a very interesting experiment for anybody to have tried upon himself. It is especially recommended to anybody who thinks that there is "nothing in psycho-analysis" and who may imagine that his mind is a smoothly working machine. After such an experiment he will—provided the list of words be sufficiently extensive—no longer be of that opinion. Full instructions for carrying out such an experiment will be found in one of the chapters in Dr. Ernest Jones's *Collected Papers on Psycho-Analysis*, as well as, of course, in Jung's book on the subject translated by the late Dr. M. D. Eder.

The mysteries as to why the author took these longer reaction times in the above instances instead of the normal two seconds, and the curious reaction words, interested him very much and strongly prejudiced him in favour of being analyzed. The author was used to trying to solve certain kinds of problems in the external world, but here were some very interesting problems inside his own mind urgently calling for solution.

Psycho-analysis has, however, explained these particular mysteries, and various others, by laying bare the causes of the respective phenomena, and thus solving the problems. Most people, including many of higher intellect than the average, seem to think that psycho-analysis is closely allied to mysticism, but the author cannot agree with them at all and can only think that their opinion must arise from an insufficient knowledge of the subject. Psycho-analysis, when properly carried out, is simply an observational scientific investigation of the mind. It is quite different from mysticism since it solves many things which were formerly mysteries; and while doubtless much remains to be solved, the final problems facing the individual are nevertheless greatly simplified.

It seems to the author that opponents of psycho-analysis and unanalyzed people are more truly the real mystics, and live with by far the greater number of mysteries existing in their minds.

Chapter Two

Experiences with Two Psycho-Analysts

THIS CHAPTER gives an account of actual experiences with two psycho-analysts from the standpoint of the patient. Previous accounts of analysis have been almost solely from the pens of analysts themselves. Criticism of various methods of analysis by analysts is not likely to be nearly so vivid as when presented by a person who is himself undergoing the process.

It will be clear from the author's general attitude that the criticisms of his two analysts which are expressed or implied in what follows are not intended to apply to the technique as devised, developed and practised by Professor Freud. People other than the author who are well acquainted with psycho-analysis consider that both the analysts who undertook the author's case made serious mistakes in technique, the first especially by refusing to allow him to develop his own thoughts as they rose to the surface of consciousness, the second by creating certain forms of hostility and discouraging any possible positive transference through hastiness and loss of temper. It says a great deal for the process of analysis that in spite of these serious errors—which it is not for a moment suggested are committed by all analysts—so much insight into his mind, and so much therapeutic benefit, were gained by him.

The author has been interested in psycho-analysis since the first English Translation of Professor Freud's

The Interpretation of Dreams appeared in 1913. In 1917, after an unpleasant time in the Army which was causing periodic slight neurotic symptoms, he consulted a doctor who partially, but by no means wholly, followed the Freudian views. This doctor advised looking at the psychic material which was troubling the author as objectively as possible and then trying to work off the effects by concentration on the affairs of daily life. The author thought that the first part of this advice was simple but probably, or certainly, rather silly as he considered that a steady contemplation of the material would certainly make him worse by reminding him of things which he would rather forget. However, much to his surprise, after following both portions of this advice, he felt much better, but was still left rather depressed and with almost complete amnesia or forgetfulness for a particular six-weeks' period of Army life—as was very strikingly brought to his attention on looking, after an interval, at some photographs taken during this period.

A dream which did much to turn the thoughts of the author towards undergoing analysis may be worth quoting. Late in 1922 he dreamt that a solid reinforced concrete bridge about two miles from his home was on fire and burning vigorously, large flames about 20 feet high springing from its south-western half. In the dream his feelings were ones of astonishment that solid steel and concrete, and nothing else, could burn so vigorously by itself, as he did not know that this was possible. However, he thought that he would not bother to call the fire brigade as the bridge belonged to the ratepayers and

7

his share of the damage would probably only be about threepence and it was worth this small amount to see and watch the unusual spectacle of solid steel and concrete burning by itself.[1] So he watched the vigorous flames with feelings of interest for some time while standing on the river bank.

On awakening, he remembered this dream but had not the slightest idea what it meant. However he had recently read a psycho-analytical article in which the author said that it was sometimes possible to ascertain the meaning of a dream by asking oneself in a very definite and firm manner, immediately on awakening, what the dream meant. So he adopted this method and asked himself, with some difficulty, in an extremely definite and firm manner, what this dream meant. Immediately his mind said in reply, "You know perfectly well what that dream meant. It meant that you were fearing in your sleep that the concrete warehouse and its contents were, or might be, on fire, but that this idea was so very unpleasant to you that you had displaced the idea on to the neighbouring concrete bridge, which did not matter to you, so that the great unpleasantness of the other idea would not be brought up to full consciousness and you could still go on sleeping"
This referred to a rather large concrete warehouse belonging to an engineering company with which the author is associated. He could quite see how he might easily have displaced this fear on to the neighbouring concrete bridge, which was of similar colour and

[1] This illustrates rather well the essentially egocentric nature of dreams.

8

material to the exterior of the warehouse and was situated only half a mile away from the latter along a straight road and would thus be very handy for the purpose of displacement. He could also easily see how the underlying feeling of fear that the warehouse might be on fire could be translated into a feeling of great interest that a solid concrete bridge could burn so vigorously, and could quite understand that he would prefer to lose threepence rather than a much larger amount of money. It was also clear to him how these two modifications taken together might enable him to continue sleeping, and the explanation seemed to be one which fitted the facts remarkably well. It was confirmed by the fact that he afterwards recollected discussing the night before with one of the other directors the very inadequate insurance on this particular warehouse; and after all this he thought that there might certainly be something in the Freudian theory of dreams and, if he had been a doubter in a general way before, he certainly was not afterwards.[1]

Early in 1923, the author decided with some reluctance (or resistance) to be analyzed. The resistance took the form that, while analysis might be good for some people, or some people might need it, and while it had in fact apparently done good to various other people whom he knew and had seemingly greatly increased their happiness, yet nevertheless it would probably not do him any good; there was probably nothing the mat-

[1] This is one of the first cases the author has heard of this very modern subject of empirical dream-interpretation being immediately put to a very practical purpose—for he at once gave sensible orders that the matter of insurance be immediately proceeded with.

ter with him really and his happiness therefore would not, or could not, be increased as a result. The latter idea was coupled with a dim realization that it might not be true and that it was possible that his happiness might perhaps be greatly increased as a result of analysis; but, against this, he had heard a lot about the pain of analysis and feared the possibility or likelihood of bad psychical disturbances and argued that " 'Tis better to endure the ills one has", etc.

The resistance against analysis took various other forms as well but was mostly on the above lines. Eventually, however, these resistances were sufficiently overcome in practice—chiefly by the urging of a friend who had been analyzed and who argued that he had become much happier as a result—to decide the author to begin analysis.

EXPERIENCES WITH THE FIRST ANALYST

The author was with his first analyst for a period of about 3 months—1 hour a day for 5 days per week. Early in this period he was so bothered by various matters which had been brought to the surface by the analytical work that he felt compelled to write them down and try and sort them out on paper, and then bring these notes to the analytical hour, read them over and elaborate them to the analyst along with any other ideas or associations which might occur to him at the time. The analyst strongly objected to this, however, and urged him to "take the cure in its perfected form", by which apparently was meant as described by Prof. Freud and other writers, or according to the ideas of the particular analyst. The author, however, persisted that he felt so bothered by what had come to the surface that he must write down these notes and bring them to read and elaborate to the analyst at this stage, otherwise he would not be able to go on with the analysis. He also pointed out that the writing and discussion of these notes were having a great therapeutic effect and doing him a lot of good. Eventually he obtained a very grudging admission from the analyst that this method might be all right, but only in the very early stages. He himself is quite certain that this method of note-writing and discussion was very good and useful at this stage in his case and that without it he would not have been able to continue the analysis at all at that time.

One morning this first analyst said at the beginning: "Have you had any dreams? We usually start with dreams," and this at a time when the author was feeling anxious to discuss and clear up various entirely different matters which had come to the surface. The author, however, persisted in discussing the various matters which were in his mind, ignoring the analyst's remark, which indeed appeared to him irrelevant and even absurd.

These instances of the therapeutic effect of allowing the patient to take his own course illustrates the importance of an analyst leaving his patient alone to do what he likes as far as possible, at least at certain stages. This analyst certainly took no heed of the Freudian maxim "to keep always to the surface of consciousness," though he made a great point of adhering to Freudian methods. Further, note-writing and discussion—even if it may go against some tenets of analysis—may be a symptomatic action associated with something else, and it may harm the analysis to suppress such a symptomatic action. As a matter of fact, the author does not think that the note-writing and discussion was a symptomatic action at all in this case, but that it simply greatly assisted the sorting out of his mind in the early stages, and certainly great harm was done in so far as this wish and action were interfered with.

The author repeatedly appealed to the first analyst to let him run on and try and talk himself out, but had great difficulty in obtaining this freedom. The analyst frequently interrupted with questions and remarks which sometimes lasted for 10 minutes or so, to the great boredom of the patient, who was always thinking of something utterly different from what the analyst was saying during these periods. He therefore paid no attention whatever to the latter's remarks but only wished to get on with his own talking in order to clear his mind of various things and anxiously waited for the analyst to cease. This analyst kept him at the analysis of a single dream sometimes for several days at a time to the exclusion of more recently arising psychic material, to his great confusion, and in direct contradiction to the counsels of Professor Freud.[1]

The author endeavoured to explain to the analyst the great good which the comparatively small amount of free talking he had been able to get in had done him, and that it was bringing dozens of unsolved problems

[1] "Die Handhabung der Traumdeutung in der Psychoanalyse.' *Sammlung Kleiner Schriften zur Neurosenlehre*. Vierte Folge, p. 378.

and conflicts to the surface the sorting out of which would have a very beneficial effect, that some had already been brought to the surface by this method and that the sorting out and clearing up of them had been very beneficial; and he repeatedly requested the analyst to make absolutely as few interruptions and to give as little advice as possible. This reiterated request was always ignored by the analyst, however, who said he was a Freudian, and that it was no use coming to him unless one was prepared to adopt the Freudian methods (whatever these might be). The first analyst also said that he knew more about analysis than the author because he was the latter's analyst, but this remark impressed the author as being absurd, and he thought the reverse was more likely to be the case, viz. that he was his analyst because in the author's opinion he probably knew more about the subject than the author. In any case, appeals to authority of this kind carried no weight with him, but left him quite cold.

This analyst also repeated several times, "Well, of course, if you don't want to be analyzed you needn't be", and this remark always used to bore the author very much, reminding him of the yokel's response to the clergyman's query, "Wilt thou have this woman to be thy wedded wife?", viz., "That's what I've come for, guv'nor."

The author tried to point out to this first analyst that some of the chief features of what is now known as the analytic process were anyhow largely suggested by a patient, or from the patient's side, viz. by Breuer's famous patient, and that this patient had to get Breuer

13

to agree to her suggested method in the first instance. The analyst would not accept this, and said that the author would know better later. The author is still, however, without this better information.[1]

The author also disagreed with the remark of this first analyst about "taking the cure in its perfected form". This remark seemed utterly unsound and unscientific—as though anything could be perfect in this world and incapable of improvement. Also if one patient could suggest the fundamentals of a method, why cannot other patients suggest improvements in it? He is quite sure that it is best to leave a patient alone to do what he likes as far as possible, the analyst saying as little as may be beyond urging the patient to talk and say what is in his mind whenever he is silent—no matter how seemingly absurd or silly or irrelevant or improper it may appear to the patient. He has since learned that the method of leaving the patient alone as far as possible —except, of course, at certain points where it is necessary or desirable for the analyst to intervene—is precisely the method that Professor Freud himself consistently employed.

After nearly three months the first analyst thought that the patient would probably get on faster and penetrate more deeply with an analyst having somewhat different reactions, and recommended him to another analyst to whom he proceeded.

[1] One is tempted to wonder whether this analyst may not have been badly soured or embittered by the mass of unreasoning opposition against psycho-analysis. The author now knows enough about the subject to feel quite sure that the discoveries of psycho-analysis, when properly carried out, are so important that analysts need not mind unreasoning and ill-informed opposition.

As indicated above, most of the results with the first analyst were obtained rather in spite of most of the latter's methods and during the comparatively rare and short periods when the patient was allowed to do as he liked, and was free from interruption by the analyst. It appears to him that the great fundamental advantage of analysis is being able to talk in absolute confidence to a person to whom presumably anything can be said, and under the influence of the mental pull of the analyst when the latter is silent. The author thinks that the "mental pull" of the analyst is one of the most important points in analysis with an analyst, i.e. when a person to whom presumably anything can be said in absolute confidence remains quiet and asks one to say exactly what is in one's mind, one tries to say what is in in one's mind, and to overcome one's resistance, in order not to appear a "dud" or a fool, with no thoughts in one's mind, in the eyes of the analyst. This the author thinks is the chief cause of the "mental pull" of the analyst—at least in his case. He is aware, however, of the essential importance attached by analysts to the emotional relation of patient to analyst, technically called the "transference". Of this unfortunately he has had little or no experience.

Before beginning, and during the first month, the author was very sceptical about analysis, but after about a month he realized that it was much better to break through any repressions in his mind, and to face reality, as he found that this method was improving his health. He quickly found that a more complete

Freudian analytic procedure was much better than the procedure adopted by the doctor mentioned in the introduction. The former tended to dissolve any worry existing in his mind into its various component underlying causes—for example into a separate self-regarding sentiment. It was not then at all necessary to concentrate on the affairs of everyday life in order to work off by other means the emotion involved in the troublesome psychic material, for it had by then disappeared of its own accord. The complete analytic procedure also has the advantage over the other method in that it does not leave one with any tendency to amnesia for any particular period or occurrences.[1]

No very deep repressions were unearthed with the first analyst, but a quantity of surface muddle and resulting worry was removed from the author's mind. His friends said that they had not seen him looking so well for several years, and his family, and brother in particular, remarked how much less irritable he was. This was not wholly, but it was certainly chiefly, due to the disintegration of psychic trouble by analysis.

With the first analyst the author found that he had various fears of his father, of which he had previously been quite unconscious. A cause of the slowing down of his speech as the result of a repression was also brought to full consciousness, and after this his speed of speech increased somewhat.

[1]The doctor mentioned in the introduction had told him not to bother about the past which was only "spilt milk." Of what use, however, is this advice to anyone who will anyhow think about the past until the complicated causes of his doing so are eventually reached and removed by analysis?

16

This preliminary analysis also caused him to realize fully, or far more clearly than before, the advisability of saying exactly what one thinks or feels to people whom one likes, whereas he had previously repressed a lot which would have been better both for their sakes and his if he had said—although they might not have liked it at the time, it would have been better for them in the end. It would also have cleared his mind and prevented the formation of further repressions in the future. This point about saying what one thinks or feels does not necessarily apply to people whom one dislikes—or where there are tactical reasons for the opposite—in that case "secret diplomacy" may be advisable in order to defeat the enemy; but the author certainly feels that the clear and conscious realization of the above point is worth more than money to him, and he is very grateful to analysis for this particular result. Of course, many people would agree with the truth of the above view, without analysis, and the author would have done the same; but after analysis he realized it so very much more clearly than before, and it was not so much a matter of doing merely "lip-service" to it. The analysis was thus a sound education in sincerity of speech and conduct.

He also discovered the chief cause of his not saying what he was thinking and feeling—a wish not to hurt other people's feelings traceable to early childhood when it might result in displeasure and possibly physical chastisement from others. It is not of course suggested that it is not often right to abstain from saying things which will wound, but merely that the author learned that the supposed desire to avoid hurting others may arise from the persistence of infantile fears for oneself and one's own safety and comfort.

The author feels certain that very many people would clearly realize various things useful to them by even only a very small amount of analysis—if not the point mentioned in the last paragraph, then something else equally useful or beneficial. Many analysts rather suggest that a lesser period than three months of analysis is not worth while, but the author cannot agree with them, for he found out the useful points mentioned above sufficiently clearly within the first month— although they were elaborated and made clearer, and other matters were entered upon, during the subsequent two months. He is quite convinced that a far longer period of analysis than three months would be well worth while and beneficial to many people, and perhaps to the mass of mankind if it were possible, but nevertheless one month only is apt to be very beneficial.

The author had heard that the number of dreams remembered usually increased very greatly when an analysis was begun, but was doubtful of the truth of this statement, thinking it improbable that a process applied during the waking life·alone could have such a very great influence upon dreams. However, when his own analysis was begun he remembered a dream of the previous night most days for five days a week for two months on end—in fact, whenever the feeling associated with a dream of the previous night was fairly fully worked off by analysis it seemed to be invariably followed by a different dream the following night. He also had one vivid "fear-of-a-lion" dream after a month's analysis—an experience he had not had for twenty years. The chief meanings of most of these dreams became quite clear to him when they were analyzed, and he was surprised to find what a lot is known, or can be found out, about dreams nowadays by applying the Freudian procedure of taking a person's free-associations in relation to them.

EXPERIENCES WITH THE SECOND ANALYST

From the first the author was rather attracted by the second analyst who clearly had his interests very much at heart, in spite of cursing him rather severely for being too polite, and wanting the author to curse him severely in return, which was done reluctantly and in a somewhat half-hearted manner. Apparently the object of this process was a training in greater fierceness, and to help to lay bare some of the causes which were probably inhibiting natural fierceness.

The second analyst also strongly objected to the writing of notes outside the analytical hour, and the bringing of these for discussion and elaboration to the analysis—in fact, he would not permit it at all. This did not matter so much then, however, as the stage of urgent need to do this (associated apparently with an urgent need for every possible assistance in sorting out muddled material lying just below the surface of consciousness) seemed to have been passed. The author mentioned, however, to the second analyst the great therapeutic effect which this note-writing method had had on him at an earlier stage with the first analyst, and that had it not been for the assistance of note-writing and sorting out at that time, the strain would have been too great, and he would not have been able to go on with the analysis, and thus would not have been with the second analyst at all. Apparently the second analyst, like the first, had the mistaken idea that note-writing, even when conducted outside of the analytical hours, necessarily leads to fixity or rigidity of ideas which, if true, would of course be inimical to analytical work. The author knew, however, from his experience with the first analyst, that this was not necessarily the case at all, for he had found that notes written down expressing ideas in fairly definite form, may lead to the discovery of something else which shows these ideas to be quite unsound and in these cases he had found that the earlier notes were then completely forgotten and discarded, but that they had served a very useful purpose in helping to lead to the discovery of something that was sound. It would, however, have probably been quite useless to attempt to convince the second analyst upon this point—he would probably have been far too obstinate, or have had too fixed ideas upon the matter.

The author once or twice tried to persuade the second analyst to permit him to experiment by trying the note-writing and verbal elaboration method with, or to, him; but this was not permitted, and the analyst added that he probably would not be so much respected by his patient if he gave way. The author strongly disagreed with this view. Being trained in what is probably a good school of scientific thought and method, he would have respected the analyst more if he had permitted him to experiment and for being an experimentalist like himself. He quite sees, however, that this method might possibly not answer with some patients.

After being with the second analyst for about five weeks the author repeated certain material several times, and the analyst instructed him to keep away from this particular material. The author endeavoured his very best to carry out this instruction and was silent for half a minute or so. Then, obeying the instruction or tenet to say whatever was in his mind (although he did not like doing so as he wished to carry out the other instruction too) he came out with this particular material again. Upon this the analyst snapped out, "If you don't keep off that material I will not carry out your analysis. We may as well end it here and now." The patient deeply resented this remark and the tone in which it was made, for he was doing his best to carry out conflicting instructions, so he rolled over on the couch, was silent for a minute or so, and felt like ending the analysis himself. However, he decided to try and keep on, for he was very anxious to be analyzed; and also he liked the analyst who, he felt sure, in spite of his snappishness, was doing his best.

The second analysis was continued for about nine weeks after that (i.e. a total of 3¼ months), but the patient's unconscious as well as his conscious was apparently deeply offended by the above remark, and not a single dream was remembered after it. Some useful progress was made in other directions and valuable information gained in actual practice, as will be seen in the next section. But the patient never felt sure that the analyst might not snap at him again at any moment, even when he was saying something which seemed to him quite harmless; and, as a result, a great number and variety of memories accumulated in his mind which he seemed unable to get off sufficiently rapidly to this analyst, although he was very anxious to keep with him if possible. However, after an interruption of a few weeks, the author decided that it would unfortunately be useless to go back to this analyst—at least for the time being.

Apparently the patient could not work off his indignation about the above remark sufficiently, or his vocabulary was insufficient, or his respect for the analyst was too great for him to be able to curse the latter roundly enough to work off the indignation sufficiently to enable him to proceed with free-associations. The author cannot help feeling that it would have been better if the analyst had said, "If only you can keep off that subject, I think we should get on faster with the analysis", that is, if he had wanted to say anything at all; but it would probably have been better if he had said nothing. If an analysand repeats anything several times this probably means that there is a lot of feeling associated with the subject, or that the subject is acting as a cover-memory for something else which has a lot of feeling associated with it; and it is probably best to leave him alone to repeat it as often as he needs, and thus break down the resistance, and release the feeling associated with it by himself. If so, this would be another instance of the advisability of leaving the patient alone to do what he likes, with the solitary exception of making him talk, and say what is in his mind, if he is silent.

The chief result of the second analysis was that a considerable amount of further worrying and conflicting material lying comparatively near the surface of the patient's mind, but of which he was previously unaware, was removed by being sorted out, with the result that his health still further improved, and any remaining irritability was still further diminished.

One day while the author was being analyzed by the second analyst, but not during the analytical two hours, the words, "Wot guv'nor—the . . ." kept repeating themselves in his mind; but he could not recover the fourth word, in spite of trying very hard. Eventually he felt so angry about not being able to recover the fourth word, in spite of repeated trying, that he thought he would have given half of anything he possessed to have known what it was, and that he would never remember again what it was as long as he lived. On calming down, he proceeded to take free-associations to the matter in the manner described by Freud[1] and the fourth word was quickly recovered as "Workus". This went back to an incident when a political speaker, speaking in an election campaign at the author's native town, said at the conclusion of his speech and as the climax: "And, my friends, let us never forget that the Unionist Party, my friends, stands for Union in the beginning (this was followed by a heavy thump on the table) . . . that it

[1] *Psychopathology of Everyday Life.*

23

stands for Union in the middle (another thump) . . .
but, above all, my friends, let us never forget that it
also stands for Union in the end (a still heavier thump)."
Whereupon a voice from the back of the hall shouted:
"Wot guv'nor—the Workus?" This remark was naturally followed by great laughter, and of course entirely
spoilt the effect of the speech.

During the succeeding analytical two hours the
patient discovered that his not remembering the word
"Workhouse" was caused by the proximity of the workhouse in his native town to the cemetery, and was related to a repressed fear of death[1] and to a repressed
fear of dying in the workhouse. Such a repressed fear
might of course lead either to greater efforts to make
money, or to a tendency to despondency, depending
upon the reaction of the rest of the personality.

One of the phantasies recollected during the second
analysis showed very clearly that when the author was
ten years old he would much have preferred to have
been very good at outdoor sports rather than to have
had any interest whatever in science (he was somewhat
interested in elementary physics at the time); and that
the diversion of any interest into any kind of science
resulted from some kind of repression upon a wish to
devote energy solely to outdoor sports. Not much
evidence was obtained as to the nature of this re-

[1] For some time the author had known that he had some repression or
other about death: thus when in 1921 (long before he started analysis) a
friend tried Jung's Word Association Test on him with an extensive word
list, his normal reaction time was 2 secs.; but, in addition to a few other
unusual reactions, he gave the following reactions to the stated stimulus
words with the stated times, viz. Dead—rotten 3 secs.; cold—dead 3
secs.; to die—rotten 3 secs.

24

pression, but apparently the author is a very natural person at heart.

Once when the author was sixteen years old he was walking from Victoria Station down one of the neighbouring streets on the pavement on the left-hand side of the road to the Horticultural Hall, Westminster, for the purpose of taking a certain University examination, and he apparently noticed the houses towering above him on one side, and he must also have noticed other things on this occasion. This happened in 1908, and a number of times between this date and the time of his first reading anything about analysis in 1913 (and a number of times subsequently), he had recollected in his waking life this feeling of the houses towering above him on this side in this road on this occasion with feelings of pleasure. Whenever recollected, the road down which he was walking, or the space above it, seemed to be in imagination a closed passage with the houses on the other side forming another side to the passage (although the sky was open). The conception of the road as a closed passage was, however, much fainter than the pleasant conscious feelings associated with the houses towering up on the one side, but was nevertheless quite distinct. Associated still more faintly, but nevertheless quite distinctly, with this conception of the road as a passage, was the vertical clock tower still standing at the Victoria Station end of this road. Whenever he recollected it the author used to wonder why he had these pleasant feelings associated almost solely with the houses towering up in the position indicated, but used to dismiss the recollection and the whole of the fainter

25

elements in the phantasy as being something quite absurd and quite without reasonable explanation—as he used to do with many other phantasies (and as probably many other people do with their phantasies) for the same reason—because he had the mistaken idea that it was something silly or absurd.

This particular phantasy came up eventually in analysis after various repressions had been removed, and the author at once wondered whether this particular phantasy of the road as a passage and the vertical clock tower at the end of it might not be an unconscious symbolization of *coitus* with the vertical clock tower as a *phallic* symbol, so, without stopping to think (in case conscious thought might vitiate the matter one way or the other) he immediately gave his free associations on the matter, which immediately flew to a pre-Raphaelite picture in the Tate Gallery of a naked woman bound to a tree being liberated by a Knight Errant with a sword. The author had seen this picture ("A Knight Errant," by Millais) in the Tate Gallery for the first time on the same occasion, and being extremely shy of sex at that period, and thinking it very improper, he had repressed any sexual ideas whatever on viewing this picture. The deeper layers of his mind had, however, apparently formulated the phantasy of the passage and clock tower in the neighbouring street, and the feeling was displaced on to this phantasy. While he remained so extremely shy of sex, his mind was apparently afraid that the sexual significance of the phantasy, or its original exciting cause—namely the picture—might become evident to consciousness if the whole of the phantasy was presented equally clearly to full consciousness, so most of it remained comparatively faint, and the whole of the pleasant mental feeling was associated solely with the recollection of the towering houses.

The author thinks this is a very good instance of unconscious sexual symbolism recollected by him a number of times in all its details (apart from its association with sex and with the picture which was repressed) during five years before he had read anything about psycho-analysis.

One result of the second analysis was that the author learnt much better ideas about analysis on the theoretical side than he had had before.

When first he went to the second analyst he had the idea that his objects in being analyzed were two-fold— (1) for the scientific interest of the matter, and in the hope of interesting scientific results, and (2) with the hope of good therapeutic results; and it is very possible that the first of these two reasons was then the more important in his mind. The second analyst soon convinced him, however, that it was therapeutic results which were the most important things in analysis, that the process had been originated and developed with this particular object, and that scientific results would come later all right if one followed the therapeutic lead.

He also told the author that it did not matter so much whether he had particular complexes or not, but that what was important was the relative strengths and intensities of the various complexes and their relation to one another in the individual mind. This was a very important new theoretical point to the author, for he had not previously sufficiently grasped the conception of the individual psyche as a complicated, but very intimately and closely interconnected whole, but had been more interested in trying to discover whether he had particular individual complexes regarded as things apart and as matters of scientific interest.

Apart from the very good therapeutic effects mentioned above, only one entirely repressed memory which would never have been thought of again without analysis was recovered with the second analyst, and that was the recollection of having his hair surreptitiously placed in curling pins by a nurse when about five years old. This was done surreptitiously because his parents would have disapproved of any such faking methods, and the author thought that he had repressed it on account of the.pain owing to their being done up too tightly.

Frequently when leaving one of the 2-hour periods the author felt happier as a result, and was glad to notice this. He still felt, however, that there was much in his mind waiting to be cleared up.

He had two hours a day for five days per week with the second analyst and found this longer period advantageous because he could dodge unpleasant material more easily from day to day in the single hours with the first analyst, whereas it was more difficult to dodge, or apparently came to the surface more readily, during the longer period each day.

From the above it will be seen that he was with the first analyst for approximately 60 hours, and with the second for approximately 140 hours. Total time 200 hours. His contentment and happiness were greatly improved as a result, and he thus considers the time and money very well spent. As indicated above, the improvement was apparently due to the getting up and sorting out in full consciousness of various previously unsolved problems in his mind. It may be mentioned that each of the analysts was a member of the British Psycho-Analytical Society.

As conclusions he would state that his experiences with these analysts led him to think that psychoanalysis in itself is a very sound and beneficial process, but that it is probably advisable for analysts to leave their patients alone to say and do as they please as far as possible, only getting them to talk and bring up repressed material in their minds—under the influence of the "mental pull" of the analyst—whenever they are silent; and that some psycho-analysts probably have a mistaken idea as to the best technique, and interfere with their patients far too much in other ways than this, to the delaying and hanging up of the best results.

The motive is clearly the honourable one of trying to expedite the analysis and it is unfortunate that more than a certain amount of interference appears to have the opposite effect. Still nobody need fear going to an analyst on account of the foregoing criticisms for it is probable that not many would interfere so extensively. In any instance of what was found to be too extensive interference, a patient could perhaps refer an analyst to the detrimental effect of this in the case of the author. A patient would then probably obtain the great advantages of analysis without the specific disadvantages that the author encountered. This has been the author's object in writing the foregoing, in the hope of benefiting the patients and thus the analytical process in general. The author has endeavoured to be scrupulously fair and feels quite sure that he is right in urging the minimum of interference beyond getting the patient to talk. At the same time it must be remembered that the above is necessarily written from the author's or the patient's point of view.

NOTE ON THE WORKING OF THE MIND

One morning when the author was with the second analyst, he finished up a long preamble of seemingly disconnected free-associations, lasting ten minutes or so, with a remark derogatory to the analyst, who replied: "Dear me, that is very interesting. It has taken all that time for you to get that out." The patient was startled by this comment for he has not been aware that the preamble had had anything whatever to do with the derogatory remark.

He therefore examined the material very carefully on his own account and was surprised to find, from the course of the free-associations in the preamble and from their nature, that the analyst's remark was undoubtedly true. When they were examined, each member of the chain of associations was clearly seen to have been a substitute formation for the thought which came into consciousness immediately after it and which the patient could not utter because of resistance, so that the substitute was produced instead. Each succeeding thought or association had gradually approached nearer to the derogatory remark against which the resistance was still stronger. Nearly all the chain of associations, and the culminating remark, had previously been quite unconscious. These facts much impressed the author for they gave him an entirely new view of the course of mental processes.

Suppose, for example, one sits down in an armchair under comfortable conditions and closes one's eyes to exclude external stimuli as far as possible. Suppose one then considers what thought is uppermost in the mind, and perhaps utters this thought aloud in a quiet voice. After this, another thought will come uppermost into consciousness and one may then proceed to utter this second thought in the same way. In the ordinary way, it might then be said that the first thought "reminds" one of the second. It appears, however, that, under these conditions, this is not what is happening in the depths of the mind, for there the process is apparently working the other way round. It appears that there are, in the depths of the mind, various vital urges and wishes which have been curbed in various ways, as by punishment in early childhood; and the ideas which have been connected with them have had large numbers of successive substituted associations built up on the basis of these vital urges and their frustrations. Each of these successive associations has apparently been produced with the unconscious aim of providing some outlet for the curbed wishes, or of hiding unhappiness resulting from the foiling of the wishes, more successfully than the immediately preceding association had proved able to do.

What apparently happens when one sits down under the conditions described is that the deep-lying urges of the mind push the first thought forward into consciousness in the hope that the second one will never be thought of consciously. So far from the first thought "reminding" one of the second as people say in the ordinary way, and as appears to be the case at first sight, it is apparently the second thought (and the thoughts and wishes underlying this) that push the first thought forward for the purpose of disguise.

Chapter Three

A Practical Method of Self-Analysis

THIS CHAPTER gives a detailed description of the method of self-analysis adopted by the author which has enabled him to recollect and recover from the ill-effects of a large amount of formerly repressed mental material of which he was entirely unaware and the existence of which he would probably have denied. It includes a severe castration complex (see Chapter 4) dating back to between the third and fourth year of life, and a very early incident closely associated with the weaning process (see Chapter 7)—the latter from the age of between 11 and 14 months. The earliest incident recollected through following the process goes back to about the age of 6 months (see Chapter 6). The fact that it has proved possible to remember such a very early occurrence as this is striking proof of the efficacy of this process.

The author subsequently found that the method of self-analysis described herein is very similar to the method employed by Professor Freud on himself a number of years ago—in particular that Professor Freud devoted attention only to the most insistent *conscious* thought at any moment; though the author's two analysts adopted methods which differed very markedly from the true Freudian ones—particularly in regard to this point of always keeping to the surface of consciousness.

Although other people have worked at rather similar

D

methods of self-analysis, some of the points mentioned in this chapter may be new, for the author thought of the particular method described and did the work entirely by himself, following it solely because he found a note-writing method beneficial while he was with the two analysts, and little thinking that the method of devoting attention solely to the most insistent conscious thought at any given moment was the proper method to follow.

It may be mentioned that an important difference between the method of self-analysis employed by Professor Freud and the one to which the author was forced quite independently, owing to his urgent need for assistance in sorting out muddled material while with the two analysts, is that Professor Freud had begun to make his important discoveries concerning dreams, and thus apparently used the method of self-analysis largely, if not chiefly, for the purpose of dream-analysis, and for making further discoveries in this field. The author however was now solely interested in the work of trying to improve his own health as quickly as he could, and with trying to work off muddled material in his mind as soon as possible with this object in view. The origins and motives of the two processes were thus quite different, for the author has never been particularly interested in the phenomena associated with dreams as such; but only in so far as these might help him on occasions to achieve his therapeutic object more quickly. This attitude may be negligent in that he may miss very interesting and important phenomena for a time; but in any case the attitude is a practical and expedient one, and it apparently leads to scientific results in the end.

A friend of the author considered that such processes of self-analysis could only usefully be employed "when one had a dream to go upon as a basis" and in reply to the author's remark that this was not necessary said, "Well, a dream anyway provides a nice bunch of thoughts from the unconscious". While this may be true, it will be found that the therapeutic effect is equally great, and perhaps more permanent, if the process is simply conducted from the ordinary level of consciousness.

The author found he was only able to follow this method at irregular intervals to begin with (about one hour per week), although he wished and intended to spend one hour a day at it. The chief cause of this irregularity was that a rather worrying military matter had persisted throughout both his previous periods of analysis, had held up the results considerably, and had still retained some of its effects. He was consciously reminded of this matter each time he intended to continue the note-writing method, and thus tended to put the latter off. This, in passing, seems to the author to be one of the chief advantages of analysis by an analyst—one *has* to attend for a fixed hour each day unless one chooses to throw one's money away.

Every time he sat down and restarted the note-writing method, he found that he could easily keep on for an hour or two. In fact, he wanted to keep on as long as possible, and the difficulty was to leave off, each of the periods producing a feeling of mental relief.

The chief difference between note-writing and analysis as ordinarily understood lies, of course, in the impossibility of a transference in the former case, and the author feared that it would be impossible to obtain such good results with self-analysis as with an analyst. It quickly appeared, however, that a transference was apparently unnecessary. He quickly obtained excellent and permanent therapeutic results by this method, and considers that it would have been difficult, if not impossible, to have obtained such results in the same time with some analysts. In any case, the therapeutic and scientific results far transcended those obtained with his two analysts, and they were obtained in far shorter time. The author feels sure that he can promise most beneficial and interesting analytical results to any unanalyzed person who will only be determined and persistent enough to follow the method.

After about five one-hour periods of note-writing, taken at irregular intervals as described above, the effects of the worrying matter referred to, which had persisted throughout and had interfered with all the previous analytical work, disappeared almost entirely, and the author found that he could sit down to the note-writing at prearranged times without much difficulty, or whenever he wished to, or whenever nothing else genuinely interfered, and the analytical work proceeded apace.

DESCRIPTION OF THE METHOD

The chief thing is that anybody wishing to work at this method should arrange to set a definite period apart for it each day—preferably in the evening when things are quiet and when one is most likely to be free from any interruptions—and to try his very best to stick absolutely to these times, and reserve them entirely for this purpose, as if one had appointments with an analyst at a considerable fee for each hour.

The next thing is to provide oneself with a large and ample supply of smooth writing paper and with a pen (preferably a fountain pen) of the kind with which one can write most easily and quickly. It is well to procure a very large supply of the good paper in order that the resistances may not have the excuse of the possibility of running out of paper if the method is persisted in, or if one writes too quickly or works at it too often. Also one may try to foster the idea that the paper may be wasted if the method is not persisted in.

On feeling able to keep an "appointment" with the note-writing method, sit down under the described conditions of quiet and likelihood of freedom from interruptions with the blank paper in front of one, and pen in hand. The method now to be followed is: *write down on the paper whatever comes into one's conscious mind at any given instant*—and this, in fact, is the great key of the method. If it occurs to one that this method is silly—write this down. If it occurs to one that it is a waste of time—write this down. If it occurs that one would like to be deeply analyzed and wonders if one has some particular complex, but is quite sure that this method will never discover it—very well, write this down.

Some apparently quite irrelevant memory may then occur—write it down. One's thoughts may then turn to some particular dream—write down what occurs to one about the dream. Suddenly, and for no apparent reason, one's thoughts leave the dream and go on to some entirely different subject—very well, leave the dream and write down what occurs to one about this entirely different subject; and then write down whatever occurs to one after that. In short, write down on the paper whatever occurs to one's conscious mind from second to second during the analytical period—no matter how absurd, irrelevant, unpleasant, never-thought-of, improper, disrespectful of the method, or utterly mad it may seem to be—write it down on the paper as fast as one can from moment to moment.

When the author was comparatively a beginner at this method, it happened several times that a memory occurred to him, going back quite a long way and with many details, and yet, before he could write down nearly all these details, some other thought or thoughts would come flitting insistently in his mind. This bothered him for the first few times, for, being anxious to get analyzed as deeply as possible as quickly as he could, he was anxious to pursue and write down the memory in question as far back as he could. After trying to do this on several occasions and ignoring the intruding thoughts, he reverted to the method of writing down and continuing the intruding thoughts (i.e. of writing down whatever was most insistent in his mind from moment to moment), and left the memory and its details entirely for the time being. Subsequently he always followed the latter method, for he quickly found by experience how remarkable it was that the remaining and deeper portions of the memory which had been temporarily ignored or passed over, always came up again eventually and usually quite quickly. Not only this, but when this latter method was followed the remaining portions of the memory, when they did come up, came up with large quantities of particular additional associations of their own which would not have been obtained if the remaining portions of the memory had been followed in a forced manner, in the first place, by ignoring the intruding thoughts. Also that these particular additional associations enabled him to penetrate deeper than the first memory, whereas if the latter had been pursued in a forced manner by the exclusion of everything else, this progress might have been temporarily held up.

Many times on various days and nights during the period when he was doing note-writing in the evenings, apparently important particular thoughts would occur to him and he would think at the time "By Jove, I must write that down during the next note-writing period". When he came to this, however, he always found that, though he was aware that the particular thought in question was somewhere in his mind floating about in a semi-conscious state, he was then never able to write it down at starting, without overcoming enormous resistance. By that time he had, however, got into the way of only writing down his fully conscious thoughts from moment to moment, and then he would eventually find that the particular thought in question came up suddenly into full consciousness—apparently from nowhere—and was then written down automatically and with no effort whatever. When this happened, he was very much interested to notice how extremely appropriate the associations written down immediately beforehand were to the particular thought in question, and that the connections of these immediately foregoing associations with the particular thought were far more acute than he could ever have thought of consciously.

The immediately foregoing thoughts frequently seemed to be of the nature of cover-memories for the subsequent particular thoughts, preventing the latter from reaching full consciousness until they were written down, cleared off, and removed. In fact the author was very much surprised to notice, during the progress of the note-writing analysis, the extent to which many of the memories of his childhood, which he had previously regarded as quite passive, seemed to be actually cover-memories for other particular incidents which had various kinds of emotional associations.

The author found that when any particular seemingly important recollection was eventually reached and written down by the process of writing down only what he was thinking of, and fully conscious of, at any moment, the emotion formerly associated with this particular recollection tended to disappear, and the recollection eventually tended not to recur again. In several instances the same subject seemed to recur several times, but only in a successively milder and milder form; but, in these cases, the author suspects that the subject was not reached the first time solely by free-associations but was partly forced.

40

This seems to have been the cause of the difference between the therapeutic effect of the notes which the author made as described in this chapter, and that of the notes which he made while with the first analyst. In the case of the notes made while with the first analyst, the actual note-writing seemed to have little therapeutic effect in itself, but when the notes had been fully discussed with the analyst, a great therapeutic effect was obtained. These notes, however, were not made by the process of free-association, but often hurriedly, and also sometimes partly in the fear that material for discussion during the analytical hour might run short. They were thus rather, or perhaps very, forced and were not free-associations, but needed full discussion with the analyst before the process of free-association on them could be started.

The author now knows that the fear of running short of material for discussion during an analytical hour arises solely through repressions; and, owing to these, one may fear that one's mind may become apparently a blank and one may fear the resulting apparent waste of time. As a matter of fact he is now convinced that one's mind is never a blank, but is always thinking of something, though one may not be fully aware of this, or of what it is thinking about, at any given time, or moment.

During the practice of the note-writing method also one's mind may become apparently a blank. In this case write down, "My mind is now a blank". After writing this down, it was always found that something or other immediately came into the mind, which was then written down. In this way, unpleasant material is approached gradually and by means of a very large number of free-associations with only gradual release of emotion. The large number of associations appears to contribute to the permanence of the beneficial results.

It might be thought that the possibility of a greater number of associations in reaching the repressed material would mean that note-writing would entail a greater time than analysis by an analyst; but the author found the opposite to be the case. He found that he could write down material which was very unpleasant to him so very much more easily and quickly in the first place by himself than he could tell it to an analyst; but that when it had reached the stage of full consciousness by the method of free-association sufficiently to be once written down in its proper order, then, after this, the feeling associated with it was not nearly so strong. Nevertheless he found it advisable and necessary to keep the notes already written locked up while he was continuing writing, in order to be sure that they were kept from other people's eyes and thus to avoid any unnecessary additional repugnance to further writing. It is also advisable to keep the notes already written locked up in order to feel that they are safely stored, and are actually in one's possession for a time (and can be read again if one desires to do so), while any remaining trace of affect, or feeling, associated with the particular material dealt with in them becomes worked off in daily life.

An interesting phenomenon occurs when all the

affect has been worked off in this manner, for whereas previously one may have been very shy of some of the material dealt with in the notes, after all the affect formerly associated with it has been worked off, one is not shy of the material any longer, and would not mind telling it to anybody.

Probably this is because while affect was associated with the material, this material remained part of one's own personality, and was thus something to be guarded; but that, when all the affect has gone from the material, it· is no longer part of one's personality and one thus does not mind at all what becomes of it.

The author determined to try dictating free-associations to an electric recording and dictating machine in the hope that this method might work as well as writing out the free-associations, and that much labour and time spent in writing might thus be saved. However, after dictating for a quarter of an hour or so to this machine, he found that this method was not having any therapeutic effect whatever or relieving his mind at all, so he gave it up. He also found far more difficulty in dictating actual words to the machine than in the note-writing of similar material owing to a partly unconscious feeling that "even walls have ears". All the material dictated to the machine came up again in note-writing immediately afterwards; which meant that the other method had not worked, and that the affect associated with this material had not been cleared off his mind by it, and apparently he might as well have dictated to a pillow, or to his desk, as to the machine.

The cause of the entirely different effect of the two methods would be very interesting to find out and the author thinks it probably arises as follows. He had noticed that he sometimes automatically wrote in his notes, for example, "Now your mind is trying to avoid something," instead of, as might have been expected, "Now *my* mind is trying to avoid something," and the automatic employment of the second person pronoun rather indicated to him the possibility that much of the effect of the presence of a second person may be actually introduced during the whole time when free-associations are being actually written down. It seems possible to the author that the actual viewing of the notes which he has just written down may bring vividly home to the fully conscious mind of a person the current of his thoughts in a very much clearer form than they were before; or, in other words, that the process of note-writing may be very similar to dictating *to oneself*, with oneself actually acting as a personal analyst; and if this be so, it may explain the remarkably and entirely different psychological effects of writing down free-associations on paper and of attempting to dictate them to an inanimate object such as a machine or a pillow. It may be that the actual act of writing also has some bearing upon the entirely different psychological effect owing to the "directional volition" required for the act of writing occupying the conscious mind, thus permitting the free-associations to flow more un-interruptedly, or far more freely, from the unconscious.

When starting this note-writing method, possibly twenty or more recollections may flash through one's mind while one is writing down the first conscious thought which occurred to one; but no matter. If the first conscious thought has been written down exactly in the manner described it is apt to be done with, from this point of view, for ever. If the next thought to be written down is the next one most insistent in consciousness, this next thought will then be apt to be done with for ever; and the same with the next thought after that. Then only seventeen of the original twenty associations remain to be dealt with; and, under these conditions, a fresh or additional association is very apt to appear apparently from nowhere. The important thing is that this fresh association is apt to be something comparatively new, and one which would never have been thought of in consciousness again without the note-writing method having eliminated a few cover memories, and having run the mind comparatively short of them. The eighteen then existing associations gradually come up, and are written down as fully conscious thoughts, and eliminated, in odd turns, and along with much other associated (and apparently non-associated) material; and, by that time, some repressions will probably have been unearthed, and an entirely new set of associations and cover-memories concealing other repressions will be present in the mind. These will gradually become eliminated in their turn and, with them, various additional repressions, releasing still other associations and cover-memories concealing still further and deeper repressions and complexes.

The method of free-association as described is very

different from the method of "introspection" which has been known and practised for centuries. Very little indeed or comparatively nothing can be done by introspection—it simply gives one a large quantity of cover-memories lying almost solely in the upper layers of the mind, and in a comparatively fixed condition, and all the underlying material remains permanently concealed. Simple introspection also may lead to worry, as one does not get behind or underneath the various points, or split them up and dissolve them, but simply runs up hard and repeatedly against the same rather sore subjects. Analysis as ordinarily understood, or self-analysis by the method described herein, is something quite different from introspection, enabling one to penetrate deeper and deeper into one's mind and to split up and entirely dissolve all superficial worrying material.

The most important thing to do in this analytical process is to endeavour to allow the thoughts to arise in the mind, and be written down, quite automatically with no attempt whatever to criticize anything or keep anything back in the first place because it is painful or "absurd" or for any other reason. If this plan is followed exactly one obtains information, or quantities of data, coming freely from one's mind, over which one has not exercised conscious control, and for which one is not consciously responsible. This material is thus outside of one's conscious personality, and from a scientific point of view is "objective" to the latter.

It is all very well, and the correct scientific procedure of course, for consciousness to be highly critical of all

46

this material *after* it has been brought forth in the completely unhindered and non-critical manner described—that is to say it is right *then* to doubt its truth as much as possible, to omit any parts of which one is not absolutely certain, and to endeavour to arrange the remainder in a coherent scheme. If, however, this quite proper highly critical attitude were adopted towards the material before it was brought forth in the first place or while it was being produced, the whole objective or scientific nature of the procedure would be lost. The essence of this method of self-analysis as a scientific procedure lies in the maintenance of a perfectly non-critical and non-selecting attitude while the material is being brought forth in the first place.

Investigation of his own mind by this process is much the most interesting kind of scientific research the author has come across up to the present; but, until quite recently, he did not know the instrument or method required for this deep penetration of, and research into, his mind; but thought that any such process was quite impossible, and that his mind must necessarily and for ever remain a closed book to him— since it was fairly apparent that only such a comparatively very little could be done by the method of intro-spection—the only method he knew. As already in-dicated, simple introspection, too, is apt to injure one's health, whereas the analytic process, on the contrary, tends to clear away repressed worry and improves the health.

It is advisable to realize fully at the start the great difficulty of sitting down to note-writing analysis, and

47

of being perfectly frank with one's conscious thoughts from moment to moment. One must not attempt to minimize this difficulty and the strength of the initial surface repressions, nor be discouraged if—like the author—one is only able at the start to keep one one-hour "appointment" each week with the note-writing method, instead of perhaps seven.

If, in spite of all this, one nevertheless does one's very best to stick at it, and at keeping the "appointments," or at working at the method whenever one can, then, fairly soon, some of the worst surface repressions will be overcome, one will find one's health and happiness improving, and get quite keen on the method, and on the interesting and beneficial results. The analytical work will then go on apace.

As already indicated, the author kept on at the method of writing down his conscious thoughts from moment to moment at first simply because he found that it was continually clearing and relieving his mind —i.e. solely for the therapeutic results. He never thought that writing down only the thoughts most fully conscious at any time, and paying no particular or special attention whatever to dreams, for instance, would eventually lead to deep analytic results; in order to obtain the latter he thought that he ought to aim at paying attention chiefly to any *unconscious* thoughts which he might have. He now sees, however, that, on the contrary, the former method is right and the best for eventual scientific results, as well as for the clearing of one's mind, i.e. only pay attention to and write down the most fully conscious thoughts at any particular moment—if they happen to be about a dream or phantasy write them down—if they do not happen to be about a dream or phantasy, don't worry, but just write them down whatever they are about, *and keep on writing down one's fully conscious thoughts from moment to moment as well and as fast as one can during the analytical period, no matter how rapidly they may wander from subject to subject and no matter how foolish, absurd or irrelevant they may from time to time appear to be.*

The author has heard that one of the chief disadvantages of analysis is the amount of the analyst's time taken, and the resulting expense, and the fact that there are far too few analysts to deal with the number of people who would be benefited by and interested in the process. It is possible that a sound and experienced analyst might obtain results more quickly than they would be obtained by a note-writing method and that in some cases—where people lack determination—a personal analyst may be essential; but nevertheless the author feels sure that, given persistence and determination, there is no reason why anybody should not become very deeply analyzed—no matter how far away he may live from any analyst, nor how impossible or inconvenient it may be for him to visit a distant town for this purpose, nor how incapable he may be of affording the usual high cost of analysis. Persistency in the first place is all that is required until one begins to notice the improvement in one's health.

The chief benefits the author received from the analysts in relation to self-analysis were the breaking down of his initial resistances and a clear and conscious

49   E

realization of the fact that *none* whatever of his thoughts were really absurd or irrelevant (no matter how much they might appear to be so on the surface of the mind) and he has already emphasized the importance of these points as strongly as he could. The apparently absurd and irrelevant thoughts arise of course owing to the operation of the so-called "complexes" repressed in the mind.

One great advantage of the method described is that people who think that they would be shy of telling their intimate thoughts to another person need not do so; but can just write down these thoughts for themselves, and keep them locked up until they have worked off the feeling regarding them. The author has already mentioned that the absence of the need of overcoming the resistance of telling each new intimate thought to an analyst, greatly quickened up the process in his case, enabling much more work to be done in the same time.

Another advantage is that one is free from the idiosyncrasies of particular individual analysts—such as the peculiarity of the author's first analyst, who tried to hold him solely to the analysis of particular individual dreams for several days at a time—no matter how much his conscious thoughts might wander away from it— to his great mental confusion and irritation and the delaying of good results.

It will be found that the getting of a large number of thoughts written down and off one's mind renders the mind clearer, and that one subsequently does the things of greatest importance first in one's daily life more readily than previously when a certain amount of confusion and repression was in the mind. The process also reduces any nervousness which may be present by eventually dissipating the underlying repressed emotion. In this respect it is much better than experimenting with the psycho-galvanic reflex or with the word-association test, for the latter processes only indicate the presence of emotion without removing it to any great extent. Nevertheless the removal of emotion is painful, and thus this method requires far greater determination than merely experimenting with the other processes.

One advantage of the results obtained by self-analysis is that they are necessarily free from the generally unfounded criticism—so common in England and America—that the analyst reads the results into the mind of his patient.

A confidential friend whom one could consult and with whom one could discuss any trouble or difficulty which might arise might be a great help with self-analysis. It is undoubtedly true that "a trouble shared is a trouble halved", and analysis certainly indicates the advisability of every person having a confidential friend—preferably his medical adviser if the latter is at all interested in the subject of the mind.

SOME PRELIMINARY RESULTS
OBTAINED BY NOTE-WRITING ANALYSIS

In addition to the deep therapeutic recollections from early childhood dealt with in Chapters 4, 5 and 6, going back to the ages of 3½ years, 11 to 14 months and 6 months respectively, it may be useful to give an

51

account of one or two results obtained in the early stages of the work. This might assist other people to judge by analogy that the process was working properly in their own cases, and thus that they would probably ultimately remember incidents in their very early childhood by continuing it. It must be remembered that the object of analysis is not the mere recollection of incidents, but the working off of painful emotion associated with unpleasant incidents. This removal of emotion cannot however usually be effected until the incidents in question are recollected: continued free-association and an abreaction then eventually brings about the other result.

Analysis apparently consists in the early stages of the exhaustion of emotion concerned with recent happenings so that the mind then thinks of something deeper or more remote. In this way a person gradually penetrates deeper and deeper into the mind and eventually obtains complete pictures from deeper levels inside the mind of the manner in which certain of the earlier thought processes and dreams had been produced, and of various stages or levels in the production of these earlier thoughts and dreams. Needless to say, these internal pictures of the former working of the mind when viewed from deeper levels are extremely interesting and instructive. They illustrate very clearly amongst other things that some of the earlier dreams had a definite causation.

While, however, in the comparatively early stages of analysis it may be found that the mind works backwards fairly uniformly, as just described, later on it will very likely be found that the mind suddenly takes a very deep dive down to a happening in early infancy, leaving a large and comparatively blank gap in between. After this the mind may perhaps not deal with the various matters in the general inverted order of their original occurrence as formerly. In such instances probably the mind had to remove the ill-effects of the early infantile occurrence before it was able to deal with the unpleasant events which had occurred later during the gap which was temporarily left blank. Anyhow in the author's case the relationship of the events which had occurred during the gap to the infantile event referred to were certainly of this nature.

The results are not obtained by conscious searching —anything of this nature would probably tend to put them in the background. They are gradually realized by the mind during the process of free-association when the thoughts are allowed to wander as much as they wish. They thus come up along with very many relevant, and apparently non-relevant, free-associations the therapeutic effect of which is far greater than that of the isolated specific results. Many of the results may seem to be pathological. However, if any unanalyzed person examines his own mind carefully by an analytic process he will be surprised at the amount of pathological material which it contains and which would be better removed. There are many apparently silly things stored in the unconscious which at the time of being stored there were decidedly not silly. The following are illustrations of how deeply lying experiences may be brought to the surface.

53

DISCOVERY OF THE ORIGIN OF AN INTEREST IN ANTIQUES

(cleared up after 11 hours)

For a number of years the author had been interested in and had collected antiques. He was only interested in those older than the usual maximum span of human life (i.e. about 80 or 100 years) so that the people who made them were certain to be dead. This interest in antiques was traced down in the course of free-associations to its earlier stages when it was confined to old oak chests such as are frequently seen in antique shops. These, he found, had represented coffins to his unconscious mind, and the interest in them had satisfied a repressed and completely unconscious partial death-wish caused by certain unhappy events which had occurred just before this interest in old chests developed. When the painful emotion associated with these unhappy events was eventually removed by free-association, the death-wish founded upon it disappeared, as also did the interest in old chests. Along with this the interest in antiques generally, *as* antiques, also vanished. The author is now only interested in such objects if they possess some quality which appeals to him other than mere age. The former *desideratum* that the object must be older than the maximum span of human life is interesting in view of the fact that the objects were satisfying an unconscious death-wish. For years before the latter fact was discovered the author had occasionally wondered what could be the explanation of the first fact.

54

Origin of an Interest in Astronomy

(cleared up after 17 hours' work)

Ever since his schooldays the author had been interested in astronomy and had purchased a small equatorial telescope which he sometimes used for examining celestial objects. If anyone had asked him the cause of this interest he would have replied that it arose because he felt that it was the duty of any educated person to know something about the latest ideas concerning the universe in which we live. This rational explanation of the interest in this subject would certainly have been erroneous however, although it would have been given quite honestly. During the progress of the free-asociations this interest was traced back through the nursery rhyme, "Twinkle, twinkle, little star," down to admiration of, and interest in, the white flowers of a specimen of the plant "Star of Bethlehem" (*Ornithogalum umbellatum*) which grew and flowered for several years near a garden in the country which he used to tend when about ten years old. The white flowers of this plant certainly looked strikingly beautiful amongst the tall green grasses of the roadside; but undoubtedly his great interest in it, and the reason he remembered it, was because of the name "Star of Bethlehem." The free-associations then immediately passed on, with undiminished interest, to the "Star in the East" and the account of the birth of Christ as given in the New Testament. Undoubtedly his great specific interest in the "Star in the East", and ultimately in other stars generally, arose as a sublimated form of a very great repressed childhood interest in the stated facts concerning the birth of Christ which had also helped to solve the earlier problem of his own origin.

A MENTAL BLIND SPOT

(Cleared up after 18 hours)

After working for about eighteen hours at the method the author suddenly remembered an occasion on which he had frightened himself rather badly by gazing up at a pair of long and sharp mounted Highland cattle horns which used to hang over a certain doorway in the house in which he was born.

He had imagined at the time how terrible it would be to be tossed by an animal having such formidable structures as these, or for one of them to be run through his body. He was between 5 and 6 years old at the time of giving himself this fright, and had certainly not thought of the incident again since the age of 7, until it was remembered by self-analysis, i.e. not at all during an interval of 26 years.

He was away from home with his brother at the time of the analytical recollection, to whom he related the original incident, remarking, "I wonder where those horns are now?". Whereupon his brother replied, "Do you mean those Highland cattle horns which hang over the dining-room doorway in our present house?" The author responded, "Are they there now?

They surely cannot be for I should have seen them", to which his brother replied that he thought they must be the same.

Upon returning home the author was very surprised indeed to find the same large horns hanging up in the position indicated, although he had not seen or noticed them consciously for over 20 years. This is all the more remarkable as they were by far the largest and most conspicuous objects exposed to his gaze each morning on coming downstairs. These facts were very surprising to the author, and the phenomenon is undoubtedly a striking instance of a mental blind spot. In spite of the fact that the horns were by far the most conspicuous objects present, his mind was apparently able to ignore their existence entirely, and he saw completely through them, as it were, to the wall-paper beyond, owing to having frightened himself with them in his childhood.

If many other people possess such pronounced blind areas, as they probably do, they would, of course, never become aware of the fact unless or until the repressed emotion formerly associated with the objects had been removed by an analytic process, or by some other method.

The phenomenon interested the author as indicating that evidence in Law Courts, for example, that certain objects were not present on a certain occasion, is not necessarily reliable. Probably evidence that certain objects were present under certain circumstances is, on the whole, far more reliable than evidence to the effect that they were not present.

A Talking-to-Oneself Derivative of the
Note-Writing Method

As mentioned already, the author tried dictating free-associations to an electric recording machine fairly early; but found that this process of dictation to an inanimate object apparently had no therapeutic effect and did not succeed in removing emotion from the material dealt with.

This was apparently largely due to a partly unconscious feeling that "even walls have ears" and to the spoken associations not being entirely free as a result of this. Also the dictation to the inanimate object did not have the same effect as the writing down of associations for oneself to see.

After about 120 hours of note-writing, however, he found that he had dealt with and completely removed the fears associated with the feeling that "even walls have ears" and after this, he could then utter free-associations to himself in a quiet room, and that this process then had the same effect as the previous note-writing, in addition to being much quicker. For some time he used note-writing alternately with the talking-to-oneself method in order to be quite sure of not missing any advantages which the note-writing might have; but subsequently he employed the talking-to-oneself method only.

The author is somewhat doubtful of the advisability of giving these facts in case anybody should feel tempted to start with a talking-to-oneself method straight away in view of the apparent saving in time by doing so.

It is therefore advisable to state that it is probably absolutely necessary, when working alone, for anyone to begin with a note-writing method and to continue this process until all the existing fears against uttering thoughts have been completely removed.

A friend of the author considered this difference interesting and thought that a lawyer, for example, would probably find stronger resistances to committing thoughts to paper than in merely uttering them. This is, however, probably not so. The author eventually found that most of the·resistance against uttering thoughts aloud in his own case came from unconscious repressed fears resulting from repressed memories of punishments, and fear of punishment, in early child-hood. These had resulted through expressing one's opinion about various matters, asking questions, etc., too frankly, or without regard to the opinions of stronger adults, and were partly a result of the general attitude that "children should be seen and not heard". Note-writing, however, unlike quiet speech, does not involve the possibility of "being heard" and it is a very useful method of getting out these particular thoughts without encountering the unconscious resis-tances, founded upon the repressed fears, which the other method involves.

A Psycho-Analytical Method of Getting to Sleep

Some time ago a well-known popular newspaper published considerable correspondence concerning various methods of getting to sleep. The author was slightly troubled by insomnia at that time, and frequently had some difficulty in getting to sleep, so he tried a number of the suggested methods.

The most successful one in his case proved to be the process of painting large imaginary figure 3's very slowly and deliberately on a large imagined black wall with an imaginary brush and tin of white paint. The author of this method had said that after anybody had painted three of these 3's in this way he would find it quite impossible to remain awake.

This process usually worked very well in the author's case. He usually went off to sleep after he had finished painting only one or two of the 3's; but, if not, almost invariably after he had finished the three of them. Many of the other correspondents emphasized the importance of thinking of pleasant things when attempting to go to sleep. Many people apparently have a feeling of pleasantness associated with the "sacred" number 3, which feeling is frequently intensified when 3 is itself used three times in producing the number 9.

Most people when asked if they have a favourite number, or what is their favourite number, will reply that they have not got one. If pressed, however, they will frequently spontaneously respond with the number 3, and may state that, after this, they prefer the number 9. In this connection one is reminded of the American millionaire, who, as recently reported, invariably bought stocks and shares in 3's, and in multiples of 3. His office was also No. 33 of 33rd Street, and he obtained 333 as a telephone number.

Many psycho-analysts would probably say that the reason the figure 3 was suggested is because of an unconscious phallic significance of this number. Unconscious phallic symbols generally have a pleasant connotation—except when they happen to be associated with the castration-complex, and then the feeling is very much the reverse of pleasant. Castration associations will, however, in practice, probably never appear when one is attempting to go to sleep, although they may sometimes be produced immediately after an individual dream.

Nevertheless the author obtained few, if any, phallic associations with the number 3 and is himself rather inclined to think that the "sacredness" and pleasantness of this number in the case of many people may frequently arise from the idea of a trinity of the individual himself and his two parents in infancy and early childhood.

Practically the only instances in which the method of painting imaginary 3's failed to result in sleep was when the author unconsciously broke off, while still awake, the imaginary painting process before three of the numerals had been completed. This sometimes happened near the centre loop of either the second or third 3. When this breaking-off occurred, he would then lie awake perhaps for an hour or two, faintly thinking of various things in a not very clear manner until he eventually dropped off to sleep.

This happened a number of times before he fully realized that, on each of these occasions, he had unconsciously broken off the imaginary painting process. When this latter fact was fully realized he wondered what could be the nature of the intruding thoughts which had caused the imaginary painting to be broken off. By this time he had developed the talking-to-oneself derivative of the note-writing method of self-analysis, so he applied this talking-to-oneself process to discover the nature of the intruding thoughts, uttering any idea which occurred to him in a quiet voice, while lying in bed, and continuing this process as long as he could.

He found that this process enabled him to discover the nature of the intruding thoughts on any given occasion; and that, on following it, he invariably went to sleep within a quarter of an hour or so, whereas otherwise he might have lain awake for one or two hours. Apparently, when following this method, the mind continues with free-associations until some heavy repression, in the Freudian sense, is approached. If one persists in attempting to follow the process when this latter stage is reached, the strain apparently becomes too great and the mind goes off to sleep rather than undertake the work of dealing with the heavily repressed material. The process has removed some of the superficial irritating thoughts, and sleep then apparently provides a good excuse for avoiding the heavy repressions. When a free-association produces a definite effect such as enabling one to get off to sleep when otherwise one was unable to do so, it is probable that this free-association was dealing with the real cause of the sleeplessness far more closely (although probably in a disguised form) than many people suppose. Otherwise why did the sleeplessness cease? This problem is not easy to solve.

In addition to getting off to sleep more quickly when the mind happens to be disturbed, some other advantages of this method are that the time spent upon it assists one's self-analysis, and one is also more apt to dream about the heavily repressed material. These dreams can be dealt with the following day, thus further assisting the analysis. Whenever the author had any difficulty in getting off to sleep he always employed this method straight away instead of bothering about painting 3's. However, since his deep analysis has been successful, he no longer has the trouble in getting off to sleep that he formerly had.

Some disadvantages of the method are that it required considerable persistency and people would probably be unable to follow it until they had some experience either of note-writing self-analysis or of analysis with an analyst. However, many people may find the method of slowly painting imaginary 3's useful.

Chapter Four

A Castration Complex[1]

THE RESULTS described in this chapter were obtained by continuing the method of self-analysis for a period of about 180 hours.

The author was originally entirely sceptical as to the general occurrence of the castration complex in the human mind, considering the idea to be very far-fetched; and certainly did not believe that it was at all likely to be discovered in his own mind. After conversation with a friend who had been analyzed, and after some personal experience of analysis, however, he came to think it more likely that such a complex might enter into his own mental constitution, especially as he had been conscious for a number of years of a slight feeling of faintness whenever he read anything associated with castration in scientific literature—such as descriptions of the method of sterilization by severing the *vasa deferentia*.

In the self-analysis his free-associations eventually led to an incident of his childhood between the ages of 6 and 7 when he pulled out one of his milk teeth in the street and was surprised how painlessly it came away. He remembered that at the moment of extraction of the tooth he was peculiarly impressed by the crack between two kerbstones a few feet away.

[1] It is to be noted that whereas in ordinary language castration means removing the testes, in psycho-analysis it means removal of the penis or in some cases the whole of the external genitalia, and the "castration complex" is based on a repressed fear of the loss of the male organ or of the external genitalia.

64

The following night he dreamed that he felt in the roof of his mouth at the back something which he was sure was some kind of internal parasite. This he took hold of with two fingers and pulled out of his mouth. It was then seen to be a definitely organized object feeling slightly alive between his two fingers, rather like an *Amphioxus* (i.e. pointed at both ends but about 6 inches long). A fish's head was faintly outlined at one end. He thereupon threw it on the floor, where it gave one wriggle and then lay still.

On awakening immediately from this dream he realized that the fish's head meant that the object was a phallic symbol to his mind and he then experienced intense horror. While the horror still lasted there flashed into his mind a very vivid recollection of seeing a butcher chop off with a sudden blow of a heavy cleaver a string of fat close to a joint of meat on a large block of wood. The details of the shape and size of the fat were very clear in his memory. Further horror accompanied this memory, which represented a real incident of his childhood, an incident which aroused at the time a fear of sudden and violent castration carried out as the butcher had cut off the fat from the joint, but which was immediately completely repressed. The horror now quickly passed off and the recovery of this memory apparently largely freed the author from a slight feeling of horror that he had felt for many years on seeing the Pleiades—known locally as "the butcher's cleaver"—especially for the first few times after their rising in the autumn. This he was quite conscious of but would scarcely admit to himself, although he had several

65   F

times vaguely wondered why it was there. After the recovery of the memory related above the author was able to look at the Pleiades with comparative equanimity, though still with a slight shivering.[1]

A little later on a long spell of free-association came to a sudden stop and the author found it impossible to proceed further. On asking himself what the repression could be which was causing this strong and obstinate resistance there came the spontaneous answer, "Castration". Finding it still impossible to proceed with free-association he hoped that he would have a dream that night which might give him more information, but he also thought that the dream must not be too horrible. "Slight traces" of a castration complex in the dream would be sufficient in order to satisfy his intellectual curiosity. At the same time something in his mind seemed to reproach him for using so powerful and dangerous an instrument as psycho-analysis, and for being so persistent. If he went on long enough he now feared that he would eventually discover something significant! He did indeed have a dream that night and

[1] This slight remaining shivering eventually completely disappeared with the raising of the complete castration complex (see later) to full consciousness and the subsequent working off of the affect formerly associated with it. This complete removal the writer considers to be sound confirmatory evidence of a causal connection.

Many people probably have from time to time similar slight but very definite feelings of horror in conscious life towards apparently quite harmless things, which they refuse to admit to themselves and would deny if questioned about, and are mostly unaware of, except at the comparatively rare moments when they are in the presence of the exciting causes, or until the matters come up in free-association; but the author's slight but very definite former feelings of unreasoning horror towards the Pleiades in fully conscious life—and the real reason of this indicated above—may be interesting to those who think that there is nothing in psycho-analysis.

it was certainly concerned with castration, but attempted free-association to it was not productive of further results.

For many years the author had recollected at infrequent intervals and with feelings of pleasure a certain walk he had taken as a child with a close female relative. All he could remember about it was that it came on to rain and that either he or the relative put up an umbrella; also that it was after this walk that he first began, at intermittent intervals, to avoid stepping on the cracks between the paving stones, a tendency he rationalized by arguing that the centres of the stones were better able to bear his weight than the cracks, and that it was therefore cruel and inconsiderate to step on the cracks. During analysis association sometimes ran on the subject of this walk, and he gradually recollected that there were some bullocks in a field on one side of the road on this occasion and that he asked his relative what was the difference between a bullock and a bull, though he knew the answer perfectly well. He was now convinced that the cause of his remembering this particular walk was an interest in castration together with what can only be considered as some kind of sexual interest in the female relative.

Considerably later in the course of the self-analysis there occurred to him the sentence, spoken angrily: "Oh, he's been doing that again, has he? Leave him to me, I'll soon cure him of that". Associated with this was an extremely dim suggestion that it was Cousin —— who spoke (not the same relative as the one referred to in connection with the walk mentioned in the preceding

67

paragraph). The associations then diverged to quite different topics. Several days later the sentence quoted above suddenly recurred, this time with full conscious realization, that Cousin —— was the speaker. The author then asked himself, "Where did she say this?" and the reply came, "In the kitchen of our house in ——, where I was born, of course. I had been taken down to the kitchen to see her by a servant." "Why had I been taken down to see her by the servant?" Reply: "For exposing my genitalia in the back room on the first floor." On seeing this the servant took hold of me by the right arm, rather fiercely, and led me downstairs to Cousin —— who was working in the kitchen. Several times previously (and once before this same afternoon) this servant had threatened that if I exposed my genitalia again they would be cut off. When she learned what had happened Cousin ——·angrily replied, "Oh, he's been doing that again, has he? Leave him to me; I'll soon cure him of that," at the same time seizing me roughly under the arms, and in spite of struggle and resistance dragging me, or letting me hang by her side, up to the back room again.

The author then asked himself, "What happened after this?" Immediately a picture flashed before his mind, at first cloudy, but quickly becoming quite clear. Even in the first cloudy picture large scissors, with sharp bright blades opening and closing rapidly and scraping against one another in the air, stood out very vividly in a sort of yellowish white cloud above his genitalia. Cousin —— forced him down on a couch which stood by the wall of this room, near the door, with her left

68

arm under his right arm and across his chest, her hand being near his left shoulder. She then told the servant to give her the scissors from the adjoining table, and shouted "Go and fetch a dish", at the same time opening and closing the scissor blades just above his genitalia. He could see, at the moment of the analytic recovery of the recollection, and subsequently, the movement of the blades and could again hear their grinding noise. Up to this instant he had not believed that they really meant to do anything to him, though he had been badly frightened by the rough handling he had received. The order to bring the dish intensified his fear, and, as the servant appeared with a brownish pie-dish, a great sickness and horror went through his soul. He said, "Don't, Cunny——" (childish form of cousin), and she snapped out, "Well! Are you going to do it again?" He was now crying, and after a moment or two turned his head to the left, away from the horror, and said in a weak voice: "No." Cousin ——, who was sitting on the edge of the couch, turned towards the servant, who gave a savage push with the pie-dish towards the child, but Cousin —— pushed it away again, saying "It's not necessary, he's given in".

The author remembers with extreme vividness every detail, but owing to the appalling horror the incident was repressed very quickly after the occurrence.

He regards the brownish pie-dish as being strongly confirmatory, because he was expecting the servant to bring a small shallow white gravy dish (which was what the word "dish" used by his Cousin apparently conveyed to his mind) and was surprised by the appearance of the much smaller deep brownish pie-dish with steep sides. The surprise of the brownish pie-dish considerably increased the fear that the castration would be actually carried out. Further confirmatory evidence was obtained when he related the incident to his mother, imitating Cousin ——'s enunciation of the sentence, "Oh, he's been doing that again", etc. "Yes," said his mother, "that's exactly Cousin ——'s style." His mother also said to his father, "It's probably an actual occurrence, you know. . . . I believe every word of what he says. . . . If he had picked on anybody else I should not have believed him at all, but, instead of that he picks on the very one with whom it is possible in the light of what I have since found out about her. She is so untruthful, too, that it is no use asking her anything about the matter".

Some more facts came to light regarding the servant. The author remembered that she was the instigator to his cousin of this threat and various facts he recalled about her—namely, that she always wore a black dress, that she was rather severe-looking, and that she always wore steel-rimmed spectacles while sewing—enabled his parents to identify her as a certain Miss ——, an unmarried person of about 37 who was in the house when he was between 3 and 4 years old and who died through fire about 6 months after leaving. She was, it appears, a dressmaker—this would account for the recollected proximity of the scissors; but before he knew that she was a dressmaker, he had remembered that there were also cotton reels and a work-basket on the table at the time, and also that the tablecloth was of a coarse plush-like material of a yellowish-green colour.

The author remembered the characteristics of this tablecloth at which the dressmaker was sitting so clearly in the analytical recollection that he was sufficiently interested to inquire the technical name of this particular material at a local furnishing shop. He was informed that it is termed "Mohair".

About a year after bringing to light his castration-complex, he gradually noticed, at odd intervals during a month or so, the existence of a tablecloth in one of the rooms in the house where he now lives which was *exactly* the same as the one which figured in the above analytical recollection. When, at the end of a month or so, he realized this fact in full consciousness he was extremely interested. Nevertheless, wishing to be very cautious, and thinking that this particular tablecloth might possibly be a recent purchase, he inquired of his mother whether this was the case. However, his mother replied, "No, that tablecloth was bought at the time of my marriage".

Apparently the author was only able to realize the existence of this tablecloth consciously after all the fright associated with the castration threat had become worked off his mind, and apparently it took nearly a year for this particular result to be achieved. Thus this was apparently another instance of a mental blind-spot similar in nature to the one dealt with on pages 56 and 57.

The author remembers that his cousin went immediately to his grandfather's house for tea that afternoon, before his mother's return, and that she did not return that evening, as was usual in such cases, leaving the servant apparently to straighten the matter out, if necessary, with his parents. Before his mother's return, and after his cousin's departure, the writer remembers standing near the middle of the room crying quietly to himself when the servant said to him, "Don't cry— be a little man". It would appear that she wanted to get the matter right, if possible, before his parents' return.

His mother subsequently remembered that one afternoon on her return while this servant was in the house the latter said to her, "He's had a crying fit." This remark particularly impressed his mother at the time as such a thing had not occurred before, and she replied that the servant must have been mistaken, such things being unknown in the family, whereupon the latter replied that perhaps she had made a mistake. His mother asked him what was the matter, but he replied that he was all right. The author has no recollection of these conversations, and thus cannot say whether they occurred on the afternoon in question; but, from the reported unique nature of the crying, it rather looks as though they might quite well have done so.

The recovery of the incident was not immediately accompanied by such acute horror as might be imagined, but mainly by great dullness and sadness. The telling of the incident to a few relatives and friends, however, apparently raised the affect of horror and the following feeling of fierce resentment to the highest pitch. For some days the author was utterly miserable, and felt himself back in the time when he was a small helpless child expecting his genitalia to be clipped off the next moment, and he had never felt so completely lonely and lost in the world before. He found his friends and relatives quite incapable of appreciating the strength of these feelings, or of any adequate sympathy. After a time the author began to recover from the intensity of the affects and was able to listen to reasonable suggestions, such as that the threat was never intended to be carried out, but was solely a threat made with the object of frightening him and curing him of an infantile tendency to exhibitionism.

He gradually recovered from the feelings of ill-treatment and humiliation as his intelligence was brought to bear on the matter. His general mental condition and physical health very greatly improved, and a former slight tendency to *folie de toucher* and *folie de doute* entirely disappeared. The former he would explain in his own case by the desire to realize that he was still alive (i.e. had escaped castration) by freshly orientating himself to the world.

His former intermittent tendency to avoid stepping on the cracks between paving stones also completely disappeared. He would explain this tendency by supposing that the cracks represent definite clear cuts recalling castration. In this connection it is interesting to remember the childish saying that "If you step on the cracks you will never have a sweetheart". The author is also inclined to believe that in his own case a general, though slight, lack of self-confidence, a subjective internal mental irritation and want of placidity tending to insomnia, and a peculiar kind of mental

73

sensitiveness relating to the teeth were all due to the castration complex (cf. being mysteriously—formerly inexplicably—impressed with a crack between kerb-stones on extracting a milk-tooth. The tooth doubtless represented an unconscious phallic symbol in this case).

In contrast with the common verbal threat of castration we here have the threat *acted*, with every convincing accessory employed. The effect of this in heightening the intensity of the complex was natural enough. The "moral" is too obvious to need comment here, but the general aspects of the castration threat are dealt with more fully in Chapter 8.

The author considers it probable that such thoughtless but terrifying "acted" castration threats in early childhood are probably far more common than might be supposed, for his cousin—while untruthful and possessing some other most undesirable characteristics—could not be generally described as being particularly vicious. Indeed, in some ways she was kindly enough.

Chapter Five

An Experience in Infancy and Its Effects

FOR SOME time before he was psycho-analyzed the author realized that his attitude towards the world was somewhat depressed—a tendency to pessimism and a feeling that the world was rather "on top" of him instead of his being "on top of the world" or at least equally matched with it. This feeling was, in a sense, quite definite, but yet in another way, very vague. After some progress in analysis, however, the feeling became clearer and less vague and he began to wonder what could be its cause. He was anxious to find out, both because of the psychological interest and also in the hope of benefit if it could be overcome.

Later on, in the course of analysis, an incident highly likely to cause a depressed attitude to life came to light, as described in the previous chapter. Even after the effects of this incident were removed, however, the depressed attitude still remained to a considerable degree. As a result of observation and enquiry among others the author believes that very many people share this depressed attitude towards the world, though they realize its existence but faintly, and could not assign any clear or intelligible cause connected with their current life or relative success in the world.

Eventually, after a period of self-analysis, and after very strong resistances had been overcome, the cause of much of this residual depression came to light. At the age, probably, of between 11 and 14 months,

75

judging from his remembered type of clothes and the fact that he could only just walk, he was sitting on the knee of a woman who was wearing a green blouse. This last fact suggests that she was a visitor to the house, since according to his mother any servant or nursemaid would be wearing a kind of uniform. The child reached up several times with both hands towards the woman's right breast. As the memory was recovered in analysis he could see his small hands and arms reaching out. Doubtless the action was associated with the fact that he had recently been weaned. Several times the woman pushed his hands back rather roughly but without causing him any noticeable pain. Eventually, however, when he reached up again she apparently lost her temper and, when his arms were nearly extended, hit them back very sharply indeed with repeated blows of her right hand, causing the child great pain and aching all along his arms, and in his hands and knuckles.

At the moment of analytic recall the author felt the pain in his arms with great intensity, so that he cringed and bent his arms under the stress. The original pain caused to the child seems to have been so great that it was repressed as *pain* and re-experienced at the moment of recall when the repression was removed. Within half a minute or so of the recall he became greatly impressed by the importance of the discovery, as he realized the extent to which the repressed pain had affected his life in certain directions ever since the incident. The feeling of injury, caused by a big strong woman to a defenceless infant, was enhanced no doubt because at the time she was regarded by the child as a substitute for his mother.

Considerable fear of the woman in the infantile situation was gradually brought to light in the analysis, and the author could not see how its effects were going to be worked off. Presently this feeling of fear changed to violent anger and indignation which seemed equally difficult to remove. To relieve this he attacked the punching-ball standing in his study, trying to imagine it was the offending woman, and hit it repeatedly so hard that it touched the floor each time. His indignation then seemed somewhat relieved, though not fully dissipated.

After 20 hours the indignation and anger were apparently worked off by the lapse of time. The author has often noticed that emotion brought to the surface in self-analysis is sometimes difficult or impossible to work off during one analytical period, but frequently dies down during the intervening period of daily life. On sitting down to analysis after this interval the associations ran on distinctly Oedipus material. Possibly some of the emotion associated with the incident described was derived from the process of weaning which had occurred just previously.

The incident was followed during the early years of the author's life by considerable fear, dislike and distrust (largely repressed) of women servants and women generally, and it seems to the author that the foundations of misogyny may easily arise in some such way.

After the repressed emotion associated with the incident described had been dissipated the author acquired

77

a very much more cheerful outlook on life than he had before. Previously the *imago* of this woman had been continually by his side, though he had not recognized its presence at all before the incident was recalled after a great number of hours of self-analysis. Only a person who has been analyzed can understand at all adequately the influence of experiences in early infancy on the mental attitude of people in later life.

The whole point of this chapter is that these blows were far harder than would have been necessary to secure a non-repetition of the action objected to—and the pain was correspondingly great. It is very apparent that some adults do not realize the delicate nature of the weak growing arms of a young infant. This topic and the practical lessons to be learned from it are dealt with more generally in Chapter 7.

Chapter Six

A Memory Going Back to the Age of 6 Months

THIS CHAPTER gives an account of an incident which happened to the author at the age of approximately 6 months which he has recollected through the aid of the process of self-analysis. Several well-known medical psycho-analysts have informed him that it is comparatively rare and exceptional for a person to recollect an event which occurred at such an early age as this, although the recollection of incidents going back to the age of a year or so is comparatively common. Before analysis he could only remember incidents going back to about the age of 4 years.

A total time of about 450 hours was spent in self-analysis before the incident described in this chapter was recalled; much of the time (about 180 hours) was occupied in removing the emotion by free-association from large numbers of relatively trivial incidents which had occurred in the last 10 years or so of the author's life. His age at the time of doing this work was 33-34 years. The incidents recollected during this first period of 180 hours did not seem to call for any independent proof, for they were solely occurrences which he could then quite clearly remember happening and which he might indeed have recollected at odd intervals in the ordinary course of life. After this period, however, his memory suddenly took a very deep dive down to the incident of the acted castration threat described in Chapter 4, the occurrence of which was previously

79

entirely repressed on account of its overwhelmingly terrifying nature. In the case of the experiences described in Chapter 5 and of the experiences dealt with in the present chapter, it is unfortunately not possible to obtain any independent evidence owing to the circumstances not being of the type which would be likely to make any very great impression upon the adults surrounding him at the time of the occurrences. The memories associated with them are, however, of exactly the same character and nature as those associated with the later incidents—most of which are capable of being independently checked. The author is thus enabled, on this basis, to make what is in all probability a sound induction that the events depicted in the still earlier clear recollections also actually occurred, and indeed there is nothing to be said against this view, especially as the events seem likely enough in themselves. Another important indication of the actuality of the occurrences lies in the strong unpleasant feeling which accompanied the recollections and the great improvement in health which followed the working off of this feeling in relation to the incidents by means of free-association.

The incident referred to in the title of this chapter was as follows: One night, when the author was about 6 months old, he was in bed at his mother's breast, lying on his right side on the left-hand side of the bed. His mother was near the middle and his father was lying near the right-hand side. The baby was busy sucking and had not by any means finished. However, about this time, his father and mother each made a noise which, at a later date, the author unconsciously realized was a conversation, i.e. when he knew what conversations were. His father then got out of bed, walked round the bottom of it and took the baby away from his mother. This was very much resented by the child, for, as already stated, he had not finished his meal and was still very hungry. However, his father picked him up and carried him back round the bottom of the bed, and set him down on the edge of the bed about half-way up the right-hand side (possibly with the intention of placing him in his cot, although the author could not remember for a long time exactly where the cot stood).

In spite of his resentment, the child was apparently quiet while his father was carrying him round to the other side (perhaps because he was held too firmly to move about much). However, when his father eventually set him down he thought, "I'll teach this big object to move me away from my mother (or food). I'll kick him very hard and perhaps he will not do it again."

The baby was quite convinced beforehand that—in spite of his own extremely small size and the much greater size of his father—he could nevertheless very thoroughly frighten his father and the feeling that he could do this was very strong. It was so strong in his own case that he considers it probable that the Freudian view that every individual, before his earliest defeat in life, has a belief in his own omnipotence is entirely justified. This is naturally of interest in view of the occurrence of stories of omnipotence and magic in fairy-tales and folk-lore where—in the phantasy life

—defeats in the world of reality may be ignored, or got round in some way or other, and one's primitive opinions and feelings can have full play in an indirect manner.[1]

The author, of course, could not have expressed his feelings in the words indicated at the time, for he could not talk and did not know the meanings of words. It is possible that he could not have thought all this at the early age of 6 months but unconsciously interpreted his feelings later on when such ideas became possible to him, though before the memory was recovered in consciousness by free-association. The author, however, feels certain that this is not the case. He feels sure that, although he could not talk at the time, the primitive wishes and feelings in his mind could only be expressed in the words indicated now that he is able to use such words. This point is, of course, an extremely important one—particularly whether the author's intelligence was sufficiently developed at this very early period to enable

---

[1] A question arises—is the primitive, or very early, omnipotence feeling really primitive? It certainly seems to be; but may this appearance possibly be due to the feeling arising so early in infancy that the individual cannot remember any actual happenings, along with the associated feelings, before the omnipotence feeling existed, even under deep analysis? May the early feeling of omnipotence possibly arise owing to the satisfaction which the ego receives following the ingestion of nutriment by suckling, and from other sources of satisfaction? One might rather think that the early sense of omnipotence possibly arises as suggested since there seems to be no *prima facie* reason why it should exist *per se*. In this case, however, the strange thing is that it appears to be quite impossible to destroy the omnipotence feeling, once it has existed or been produced, by reversing the processes of satisfaction (i.e. by disappointments of the reverse nature to the satisfactions indicated); but physical punishment appears to be absolutely necessary to achieve this result. This fact rather tends to indicate that the feeling of omnipotence really is primitive after all and a fundamental underlying attribute of the ego.

him to think, or argue, that, if he could only kick his father hard enough, the latter "perhaps would not do it again." The author himself was almost incredulous of this possibility from the first on realizing that his mind and free-associations in the recollection said that he most certainly did have these exact feelings at the time of the occurrence. Realizing the great importance of the matter, and being incredulous of the possibility, the author immediately looked into the question in the most careful and critical manner of which he was capable. He has since done so a number of times on many subsequent occasions on account of his surprise and critical doubt. Nevertheless the result is the same every time. On looking right back into his mind down to the time of the occurrence and examining the recollected details in the occurrence immediately preceding the thought in question most carefully and endeavouring to eliminate any possible errors of "intrapsychical parallax" by every means he can think of, he finds that he most certainly did have the thought in question, preceding and during the details in question, although he could not have put this thought into words at the time.[1]

It will be noticed that the author's early thought involved *foresight*. It therefore appears that foresight exists in the mind at a much earlier age than is generally realized. Professor Tansley has suggested to the author that the conception of "instinctive foresight" would account for it—the power of such foresight being instinctive and inherited.

[1] *See footnote on next page.*

In any case, the fact of his father removing him from his mother, carrying him round and setting him down in the position indicated; and the occurrences described in the subsequent paragraph, and their effects, admit of no doubt, for the author's recollection of their actually happening is perfectly clear and definite

[1] This reminds one of the finale of a speech of Hilarion's in Gilbert's Princess Ida," viz.:

"These were my thoughts; I kept them to myself,
    For at that age I had not learnt to speak."

It is not always well realized how very greatly the intelligence and observational and thinking powers of normal very young infants between, say, 8 months and 2 years of age, are in advance of their powers of speech. Nevertheless a few moments of serious contemplation will convince anybody that their intelligence must be extremely highly developed beforehand for them to be able to distinguish between the meanings of different words apart from the difficulty of being able to utter them. The author was interested to notice this fact in objective observation of his little niece subsequent to the writing of this chapter. This child, at the age of $11\frac{1}{2}$ months, had evidently been able to form the induction that the handling of an occasional bottle of alcoholic liquor and a corkscrew in a certain manner by the author would be followed by a somewhat alarming "pop." Although the process was conducted some distance away, she would watch it with intense interest and, at a certain advanced stage of the proceedings, would always bow her head and hide her face and eyes with her hands, displaying signs of great agitation, until the "pop" was over, when she would immediately become normal again. On the other hand the only words she could say at this period were "Dad-dad," "Mam-mam," and "Bab-bab" in a high and hurried treble. It was found that she would not behave in the above manner at all if the same procedure was gone through exactly but with a bottle containing red tomato sauce substituted for the other kind.

This child had occasionally been given small quantities of honey, and at the age of $5\frac{1}{2}$ months, she could identify the jar which contained the honey on the table. Whenever it was raised she cried out and displayed very definite signs of wanting some of the contents. This did not apply at all when any other somewhat similar-looking object on the table was raised.

It appears probable that children are fully conscious in their waking moments comparatively soon after birth, and that some of the reflexes and other phenomena which may be observed in them at this early period are not at all "unconscious" phenomena as used to be supposed to be the case. The subsequent blankness of the early period appears to be due to "repression."

84

(see the remarks, later in the chapter, on the difference from a phantasy).

Thus when his father set him down on the opposite side and he was lying on his back he kicked out violently and repeatedly upwards at his father. His father watched this demonstration for a few seconds and then, apparently perceiving how hostile it was, determined to put a stop to it. In any case, he gave the baby what seemed to the latter to be a fairly heavy slap with the open palm of his right hand about half-way up the body on the left side. It is possible that this slap may have been intended as a caress with the object of pacifying the child, for the author is sure that adults sometimes do not realize how delicate the bodies of small infants are. The child was extremely disappointed about this result—that his father could apparently hurt him while he could not hurt his father at all. It was a great defeat—much the worst which had occurred up till then—to the former feeling of omnipotence. The baby felt too surprised and disappointed to cry. Very shortly afterwards the incident was completely repressed, along with a number of associated feelings, until it was eventually recovered by psycho-analysis.

It was apparently the author's first defeat in life, and the repression of it acted as a basis for various neurotic manifestations in later life, many of which were traced down to it by psycho-analysis and gradually disappeared one by one in the process. It would take too long to give an account here of certain reactions which the author had noticed in himself in fully conscious life before analysis and which immediately dis-

85

appeared. He had often wondered what could be the explanation of these reactions—they only became explicable on the basis of this early occurrence. Many of the phantasies which came up during the process of analysis and which were evidently founded on this incident—such as lying on one's back kicking upwards at a man whom one did not know—also became explicable on the same basis. The occurrence described in this chapter is not a phantasy, however. Only those who have had experience of very many phantasies of various types and of thousands of actual recollections in analysis can know how great the difference is between them. In particular in the author's case, the details which are present in the recollection of an actual incident are very much more sharply cut and clearly defined than they ever are in any one of the many types of phantasy of which he has had experience. In all of the latter details are usually absent or, when present, seem very blurred and indefinite and seem to carry with them a sort of subjective quality, whereas, in the recollection of an actual incident, the details seem to have no subjective quality whatever, but give, on the other hand, an extremely vivid sense of objective reality. Also, in doing research work into or upon what eventually proves to be a phantasy details have usually to be searched for, whereas, in the recollection of an actual incident, the details eventually come up in a sort of external manner—"hitting one in the eye," as it were—and the research becomes the comparatively simple matter of recording these external details and one's own subjective reaction to them. Doubtless owing to this fact, the mental feeling which accompanies the recollection of an actual incident is of an altogether different kind from that which accompanies the recollection of a phantasy. It is also far more difficult and takes far longer to recover from the ill-effects of an actual incident than from the seeming ill-effects of any particular phantasy—probably because the memory of hard and unalterable external reality is present and has to be dealt with in the former case. On the other hand any particular phantasy is merely founded upon a distorted version of earlier incidents (or of feared, or wished-for, possibilities) and can, and does, shift and change its character as the work proceeds. This does not apply at all to the recollection of an actual incident.

The author eventually remembered the incident happening as clearly as he might remember an occurrence of yesterday. Indeed, it seems to be the unpleasant episodes which make the deepest impression upon one's mind—even although they may be repressed and forgotten. The repression of such painful incidents is doubtless the chief cause of the remarkable amnesic (sometimes entirely blank) period of one's childhood to which Professor Freud was the first to call attention. The presence of this entirely blank period is itself an extremely remarkable and important phenomenon in view of the reported great intelligence of many very young children. From a critical or abstract point of view (for example, from the point of view of a still younger individual) it certainly needs far more explanation than the possibility that a person should be able to remember an extremely important and unpleasant

87

occurrence which happened to him when he was already 6 months old.

Probably the difficulty which unanalyzed persons have in seeing this fact arises from the possibility that instances of such early recollections unconsciously remind them of the many painful and repressed incidents of their own early childhood. They thus turn away from the fact and are unable to see it.

It will be noted that, apart from the author's present clear conscious recollection of their happening, the events described in this chapter are intrinsically likely to have occurred and to have had the effects stated. In fact, when he related the incident to a medical friend, the latter said, "It's exactly what a child would do—they're vicious little beggars and will kick like anything." This is a confirmation, in a way, for the author knows little about infants and would consciously have thought that he would have attempted to strike his parent with his hands whereas the memory says "kick" so definitely, violently, and unequivocally. With regard to the date of the occurrence, the author remembers that it happened, what seems to him, a very long time probably several months, before he was finally weaned and the weaning was done (according to his mother) when he was 9 months old. However, the incident might have occurred at any time between the ages of about 5 and 7 months or so owing to one's knowing very little about the time-scale at this period of life. The author has mentioned 6 months as being what seems to him his most probable approximate mean age at the time of the occurrence. It may be mentioned in

passing that he was apparently intellectually somewhat precocious in that his relatives say that he could
talk well before the age of a year.

It is certainly very interesting that such a young
child can conserve such a complexity of physical and
mental experiences. Although the author has worked
at self-analysis for approximately six times as long as
when he first recollected the above incident he has not
remembered anything earlier in his life as a result.
Nevertheless he recollected a number of further details
regarding the above incident—such as the exact position of his cot. While he cannot remember actually
being placed by his father in this, he can nevertheless
clearly remember lying in it shortly after the incident
occurred. It is undoubtedly true that most memory
depends for its existence on what we call "interest".
Investigation shows that all children are interested in
food, although sometimes not allowed to talk about it
much because it is thought to be greedy. Children are
far more closely in contact with reality than many
adults imagine.

Some readers may find it difficult to believe in the
amount of anger that was aroused in the author by the
early interference with feeding dealt with in this chapter.
However, anger at any interference with feeding seems
to be very common in animals as well as man. For instance the author bought a few years ago a black cocker
spaniel puppy "Sally". Shortly afterwards, on his
passing a table in a certain room the most terrible and
vicious doggy language came up from beneath it—
snaps and snarls and growls of the most savage and

worst possible kind. The anger and energy behind the language were so great that, although the author's mind was fully and deeply absorbed at the time in subjects about as far removed from psychology as anything could possibly be, they nevertheless instantly strongly reminded him of his own very violent anger and indignation at the time of being removed from his mother's breast when he was so hungry. Investigation showed that Sally had a large bone under the table which she was gnawing vigorously and apparently trying to eat before anybody could get it, and the trouble apparently was that the author had walked too close to this valuable object. Her anger and indignation at the possible danger of losing her food was expressed in such a way as to make the author believe that she was feeling exactly what he felt at the age of 6 months when his father interrupted his meal. The fierce anger and resentment seemed exactly the same. Although only about 8 inches long at the time, the puppy appeared to be highly intelligent at the age of 3 months, and apparently feared that she might lose her treasure, but that, if she showed her great anger at this possibility well in advance, animate objects might be duly warned and keep away from it.

On the ground of his experience of Sally's great intelligence both as puppy and adult, the author believes that she not only felt as he felt but probably also thought as he thought. In both cases it seems that the thought involved foresight—the power of such foresight being instinctive and inherited. However, familiarity with bad language apparently breeds contempt, for subsequently another person walked considerably nearer to another bone whereupon Sally immediately rushed at her ankle and drew a considerable quantity of blood from it. This must have been painful, for the milk teeth of a cocker spaniel puppy are as sharp as needles. Several people have informed the author that they have noticed similar behaviour in puppies before they have been "corrected".

The author is aware that it is impossible to refute the criticism that one cannot argue directly from the thought of a human being (even a baby) to the possible thought of a puppy. He can only say that the evidence of essential similarity both of anger and action is to him very strong. This similarity between the reactions of a cocker spaniel puppy's and his own infantile mind is one of the most interesting things the author has met in psychology. In spite of the solipsism of the behaviourists, no deeply analyzed person can have the slightest sympathy with the view that "animals do not think because they are creatures of habit". There is no wonder that a man may be so fond of his dog when there appears to be such a deep underlying similarity in the fundamental reactions of their two minds, although this may be normally unconscious in their adult years.

While the author is extremely grateful for Professor Tansley's conception of "instinctive foresight" as it seems to him to offer some reasonable explanation of his definite extremely early thought yet, nevertheless, on his thinking the matter over for several months, he rather doubts whether the foresight is really "instinctive" in itself, although the power of the foresight is instinctive and inherited and foresight undoubtedly exists at a much earlier age in the human mind than is generally realized.

The author is rather prejudiced in favour of the instrumental theory of knowledge—the view, of course, that all knowledge possessed by the brain is acquired through the agency of instruments—the eyes, the ears, the nerve endings in the finger tips, the taste-organs in the tongue, and the like—and it seems to him probable that he (and also Sally) had had earlier unpleasant experiences of separation from food following the approach of animate objects, although he cannot recollect them, and that his mind had argued that "what has happened before is likely to happen again" and was eventually moved to take steps to prevent it. On this view the foresight would arise owing to a strong instinctive and inherited tendency towards inductive reasoning on the part of the minds of some of the higher vertebrates rather than to its being instinctive in itself.

· It seems clear that, even in the deeper layers of the minds of the higher vertebrate animals, it is only relative motion which matters, for it seemed to make not the slightest detectable difference, from the point of view of producing anger, whether the author was removed from his food, or whether Sally feared that her food might be removed from her unless adequate precautions were taken to prevent this.

Chapter Seven

On the Psychological Importance of Slaps and Blows in Early Infancy

THE MENTAL effects lasting all through life (in the absence of analysis) caused by physical blows and slaps which may be light in themselves but heavy to the child, in early infancy, the author may perhaps claim as a psychological discovery of his own. It would, in any case, appear to be one of great importance.

Although many people must have got very near to it,[1] the author does not remember having seen the matter stated in any of the many psycho-analytical books he has read, which include all the most important ones. Even in Professor Freud's writings—as far as the author recollects—one meets with such phrases as "earlier tendencies are given up by the child owing to having become obnoxious in the light of later development"; and Ferenczi wrote (*Stages in the Development of the Sense of Reality*): "The outstretched hand must often be drawn back empty, the longed-for object does not follow the magic gesture. Indeed, an invincible hostile power may forcibly oppose itself to this gesture and compel the hand to resume its former position."

Ferenczi, however, wrote only of a hostile power which merely compelled the hand to resume its former position and said nothing of blows and slaps upon the hands, the effects of which travel along the weak growing arms producing great pain therein with result-

[1]This chapter was originally published in *The Psychoanalytic Review* for Oct., 1927, the author having made the discovery in 1924.

93

ing very powerful and permanent effects upon the mind. The former wish, and wish tendencies, which the outstretching of the hands was intended to gratify, become repressed into the unconscious part of the mind as a result of this pain, and the "reaching out" and similar processes tend not to recur. This is, of course, the object of the blows and slaps. The mere mental idea of the original wishes which caused these early "reaching-out" processes then becomes highly "obnoxious" to the child owing to the permanent unconscious memory of the pain—fundamentally as a result of the early slaps—which resulted from the earlier attempts to gratify these wishes.

The desire to keep the memory of this pain repressed is apparently the fundamental origin of the Freudian "censorship" in relation to many social matters. This appears to be an observational result and not a theory. The mind turns away from, and wishes to avoid entirely, the consideration of all wishes and ideas the attempted carrying out of which in the past has been followed by physical punishment, and the attempted carrying out of which in the future it is feared would be followed by punishment—this fear resulting largely, if not solely, from conscious and unconscious memories of punishments received in the past. Thus the censorship operates upon all these ideas and groups of ideas. The author's investigations indicate that the earlier wishes frequently do not become "obnoxious in the light of later development" in nearly such a passive way as practically all the psycho-analytical writings would suggest. Indeed, a few moments' reflection will show the probable importance of the mental effects of blows and slaps, for example, upon the etiology of the Oedipus complex. The memory of one's own infantile tendencies and reactions shows that the infant would naturally repeatedly and continually attempt to carry out the wishes associated with the development of this later complex until he was prevented from doing so any more owing to the effects of some form of physical punishment, when these wishes would become repressed along with the memory of the pain of the punishment, that is to say, if these particular wishes ever came to consciousness at all, and the infant attempted to fulfil them. In many cases (as in the author's) the conscious existence of these specific wishes may have been precluded in the first place, and the infant may never have attempted to carry them out, owing to the effect of the "censorship" acting upon the unconscious memory of punishment administered for the attempted carrying out of still earlier wishes of a somewhat similar nature.

The usual punishment for attempting to carry out primitive instinctive wishes, the expression of which is highly objectionable to the parent or other adult in charge of the infant, would probably be some form of chastisement. This fact seems simple enough when looked at from the point of view of an adult "correcting" an infant or young child. When approached from the point of view of the infant, i.e. from that of the adult being analyzed right down into the depths of infancy, it is a different matter. It then becomes a very difficult research subject requiring much labour and persistency, owing to the great strength of the "censorship" and the heaviness of the repressions resulting from the physical pain which these corrections are apt to cause to the child at the time of their administration. The disappointment at the non-fulfilment of the wishes also adds greatly to the strength of the repressions.

Some form of action other than slaps or blows may be adopted by an adult as punishment for a childish offence or to secure obedience. For example, a child may be sent to bed or shut up in a room or cupboard. Physical compulsion or restraint of this kind is no doubt felt by the child as the work of an overwhelming hostile force, but does not, in the author's experience of his own analysis, have at all the same permanent mental effect as the pain resulting from an early slap or blow. In the first place, punishment or the enforcement of obedience by physical restaint is usually adopted not in infancy but after the age of 3, whereas blows and slaps are used as a corrective, or supposedly corrective, punishment from as early an age as 6 months. In a child of 3 years and over the result is mainly one of resentment at losing its liberty which quickly passes away on regaining the liberty. There is no question of losing its feeling of omnipotence, as by the time a child has reached 3 years this has normally long since been destroyed or at least seriously impaired. An infant, however, may still have the feeling of omnipotence—hence the far deeper, more serious and lasting, effect of the slap or blow. It is during infancy itself, while this feeling is still unimpaired or relatively unimpaired, that slaps or blows actually involving pain are so significant when they frustrate primitive wishes or impulses, and it is this pain which, in the author's experience, is the chief source of the repressions in infancy which are so significant.

From a practical point of view this chapter is mainly concerned with the effects of physical punishment administered during the infancy period before the age of 2 years. The subsequent period, say until the age of 6 or 7 years, might be termed the "period of early childhood," and it is very important that the different effects, in practice, upon infants and children should not be confused, though effects similar to those produced in infants may also occur in early childhood. Thus a young child whose primitive feeling of omnipotence has not been too much impaired would resent and resist being shut up in a room, or being forced to go to bed, and some form of physical pain would have to be given to it in order to secure compliance, or to prevent attempts to escape. A painful accidental twist of the arm, for instance, while shutting the child up, might eventually occur and might have this effect. Some of these sources of physical pain, associated with compulsion, may be unrealized and unnoticed by the adults causing them at the time of their occurrence, although interpreted as stated by the child's mind.

The author discovered the lasting mental effects of physical blows and slaps in his own case, *de novo*, and in a very painful practical form (see Chapter 5). The pain, and resulting fear, caused by the incident referred to had remained repressed in his mind for thirty-three years and had profoundly affected his conscious conduct in many directions during the whole of that period. After this incident, he was unconsciously afraid of having anything more to do with the feminine body.

The author's insistence on the great mental importance of the effects of slaps and blows in infancy is not intended to minimize the importance of the very widespread, and perhaps practically universal, castration complex—that is to say, the great mental importance which those acquainted with the results of analysis attribute to the 'castration complex. In the one case we have a "cutting-off threat" (as a punishment and deterrent, from one source or another, for infantile exhibitionism and handling of the genitalia), and in the other case the effects of concussion. What makes the castration complex so serious, however, is undoubtedly the fact that the small child *knows* that the adults making this "cutting-off threat" have the *power* to carry it out, and could easily do so. It is this fact which causes the castration complex to have its great and extensive mental effects and for it to be so heavily repressed. Otherwise, if the child did not *know* that the adults making the threat had the power to carry it out, or if, on the other hand, he knew that they had *not* the power to carry it out, there would be no effectiveness whatever in the threat, and the castration complex could not exist.

Now, *how* does the small child know that the adults have this power to carry out the castration threat? This question may appear to many people to be unnecessary for they may argue that it is quite obvious to any external observer that the one or more far stronger adults making the castration threat against the small

98

child have the power to carry it out. However the author can only regard this view as being far too facile and superficial, for his investigations tend to confirm the Freudian view that the very young infant has a belief in his own omnipotence: the author clearly remembers that he certainly had such a belief when he was about 6 months old, as described in Chapter 6. Now how is this primitive belief destroyed or so rudely shaken? In the author's case it was by means of the mental effects of the slap which he received from his father· when about 6 months old, as described in Chapter 6. This slap hurt the baby considerably and, in conjunction with the other circumstances, served to destroy his primitive feeling of omnipotence. Doubtless earlier disappointments—for example, in connection with feeding —had occurred, but these, apparently, had been quite unable to destroy the primitive feeling of omnipotence. Apparently some form of definite physical blow or slap was absolutely necessary to achieve this particular result. This phenomenon was so marked and definite in the author's case that he can only think that it must be of universal application. He finds it difficult to believe that other people's minds can be so different from his own as a difference in this particular respect would imply.

It might be thought that many ordinary events—not necessarily hostile forces—such as not being able to reach something high up, or not being able to break some strong toy, would destroy, or would be able to destroy, the primitive feeling of omnipotence. But in fact they do not. Perhaps the difference may arise because such events do not touch the child's personality so

99

intimately, and possibly the child thinks: "Oh, well, I cannot do that for the moment but this is simply because I cannot think of the right way to do it. If only I could think of the right way, I could do it easily."

On the other hand blows, and the pain caused by them, from powerful adults in the external world are in an altogether different category. Here external reality is being *active* against the infant, who finds, by experience, that it is impossible to retaliate effectively. Such slaps thus apparently destroy the primitive feeling of omnipotence ; and, owing to the repressed memories of the physical and mental pain produced by these earlier defeats, the infant knows that the adults have the *power* to carry out the later castration threat. Previous experiences of the pain caused by these physical blows and slaps give him good reason to know the pain that adults can cause him, and these previous experiences of pain at the hands of adults doubtless increase his fear of what the pain of the threatened castration operation will probably be like, in addition to the feared loss of the genitalia.

Thus the bearing of the mental effects of physical blows and slaps and previous "rough handling" generally upon the laying down of the castration complex will be clear. They seem to be essential prerequisites for the production and existence of the castration complex, for otherwise the individual would have a belief in his own omnipotence, and he would not believe that anybody would have the power to carry out the castration threat. Probably the extent and severity of the total amount of "rough handling" (its integrated value, as it were) which has occurred up to the time of the castration threat has a very important bearing upon the extent and severity of the fright and resulting mental damage caused by the castration threat—and thus upon the severity of the resulting castration complex.

It will be noticed how neatly the independent points dealt with in this chapter bring the Freudian view of the individual's primitive belief in his own omnipotence into line with the other Freudian view of the later existence of the castration complex in the individual—i.e., into line with the possibility of the later existence of something which is quite the reverse of a primitive feeling of omnipotence.

Doubtless the effect of early blows is far greater when, as frequently happens, adults "lose their temper" with infants and children and give far harder blows than are necessary. Such occurrences as the following are within everyone's experience. The author recently heard a mother shout out to her small daughter, apparently about 3 years old, who had stumbled and partly fallen owing to being dragged along too quickly, "I'll push yer fice off if yer do it again. Stoopid little 'ussey."

It is not the pain alone of the slaps which does the harm to the subsequent adult; but the fact that this early pain has wounded the personality and has produced early twists or deflections in the individual's mind which afterwards render him unconsciously afraid to follow various courses of action which he would otherwise biologically or instinctively follow under various later circumstances. It is the cumulative effects of the repression of these numerous later thwart-ings (resulting from the internal inhibitions)—for example, upon the wish to maintain the primitive feeling of omnipotence—which does the harm to the eventual adult, although the pain of the early infantile punishments is ultimately responsible for the subsequent neuroticism, since it is the underlying cause of the primary twists in the mind. It is the memory of the combined physical and psychical pain that is so strongly repressed and, because it works continually in the unconscious, may distort the whole of the individual's attitude to life and cripple much of his activity. The actual physical injury caused is of course usually quite slight and transient though the physical pain inflicted is likely to be much greater than the adult realizes owing to his great strength in comparison with the frailty of the infant. The psychical injury, however, is likely to be far more lasting and complicated than either the physical pain of injury.

The author considers that the physical pain of the infantile punishments must certainly be placed first. It is undoubtedly extremely important. Also it comes first historically to the individual and its intensity is of primary importance in relation to the repression of the early instinctive wishes. The psychical effects on the infant then follow, and are vital for the pathological effect; and the unconscious memory of the physical pain must therefore be repressing some important instinctive wish, the carrying out of which is really vital to the health and happiness of the individual either in infancy or in later life.

A fierce attitude on the part of the adult certainly enhances the effect of the punishment, after pain has once been administered, for it increases the likelihood of further pain. On the other hand, the author found that a pleasant manner while administering pain did not diminish in the slightest degree the effect of any pain actually administered.

It might be thought that subsequent kindness on the part of a mother, for instance, might possibly undo the ill-effects of earlier punishment, whether caused by herself or by somebody else. This is, however, apparently not the case at all. If the pain was sufficient, as it is very apt to be, it tends to become repressed on its own account in the infant's mind, and, in any case, part of it would probably become repressed. Subsequent "kindness" in itself is then apparently powerless to touch, reach, or remove the repressed material, which can probably only be reached by means of psycho-analysis. The author quite clearly remembers that his cousin, when she realized that she had gone too far, and the dressmaker subsequently (before his parents returned) tried their very best by kindness to undo, or at least cover up, some of the effects of the castration threat. However, the author also remembers that this did not undo the effects of the castration threat in the slightest degree. "Kindness" afterwards only caused it to be buried more deeply.

A distinguished scientific friend said to the author that he did not think that this chapter was of much practical importance because he considered that "It is probably quite impossible to bring up a child to be eventually a civilized human adult without slaps or physical punishment of some kind in early infancy". It may be mentioned, however, in passing, that we are here not primarily concerned with the practical importance of anything, but solely with scientific research. In this respect the above opinion confirms the scientific importance of the matter, for, if slaps or physical punishment of some kind are apparently so essential to turn an infant into a civilized human adult, it seems to be a necessary corollary that these slaps in infancy must have some great lasting effect of some kind all through life.

It is probably true enough that it is quite impossible to bring up an infant without slaps of some kind, but, from the point of view of the infant's subsequently having a happy life, it is very important to be sure that these slaps in infancy should always be as light as possible, and that the frail physical condition of the young infant in relation to the strength of adults should be thoroughly realized. This point is of great practical importance—particularly with regard to the matter of leaving infants and young children alone with possibly unreliable people. These, it should be realized, have not the same interest in them as have normal parents. Parents also however would do well to remember the importance of the matters referred to, though this would generally mean in their cases not losing their tempers with their children and giving too hard blows.

A distinguished biological friend of the author who has been partially analyzed and who has an extensive knowledge of psycho-analytical literature said to him,

"You have too great an idea of the mental importance of the pain caused by slaps and blows in early infancy in thinking that it is so very important, although, of course, such slaps in infancy are very important in that they confirm tendencies which are already present in the child's mind".

Taking however, for example, the hypothetical case of the small child referred to on page 109 it seems only reasonable to suppose that this small child would have gone on talking, as before, if it had not been for the effects of the slap received from his father. In other words the cessation of the talking was doubtless entirely due to the effects of the slap, and this slap did not by any means "confirm a tendency already present in the child's mind", for entirely the opposite tendency was present before the slap was given. The author does not agree with his friend's point of view at all, for it undoubtedly runs counter to certain easily noticed facts of observation.

The author has met a number of instances in his own life in which a "feeling of guilt" associated with actions harmless in adult years has turned out, upon analysis, to have depended upon the psychic effects of punishment, and threats of punishment, for similar actions in earlier life, although other influences and tendencies, operating in the interval, had elaborated the feeling.

An interesting subject, from the point of view of analytical theory, is that nobody can say, without specific investigation of the matter, that these early infantile punishments are not one of the essential conditions for the production of such phenomena as the "super-ego" or "ego-ideal" in the adult mind, for such early infantile punishments always occur and produce a partial splitting of the primordial personality. On this view the primitive condition of the infant's mind, before the occurrence of such early infantile punishments, would be far simpler than it would be if the super-ego and similar complicated phenomena were supposed as pre-existing in the infant's mind. The latter possibility seems a very improbable one to the author.

One reads far too much about certain actions and the satisfaction of certain instincts· being repressed *because* they conflict with the individual's "cultural ideas". It should not be forgotten that the very young infant has no "cultural ideas" at all and that these arise subsequently—in the author's view—on the basis of the mental after-effects of early physical punishments in bringing about the early partial repression of various instinctive wishes. The particular form or manifestation of the underlying instinctive wish becomes repressed, along with the pain, in the mind, in a sort of combined form, or very close mixture, so that any tendency to carry out the wish in the future unconsciously reminds the individual of the repressed pain; and the possibly very important wish is prevented from ever being carried out satisfactorily, or naturally, with possible resulting very bad effects indeed upon the individual. The important thing, for avoiding subsequent neurosis, and possibly later psychogenic insanity such as melancholia, is that these early infantile deterring punishments, in relation to the instincts, should not be too strong.

Blows or slaps do not need to be at all frequent provided they are sufficiently painful physically and psychically to the infant when they do occur and are operating against powerful instinctive wishes, and indeed they may be very infrequent. For instance, severe slaps or blows only occurred on two occasions in the author's infancy—at the ages of approximately 6 and 11 months, respectively. Nevertheless this was sufficient to arrest completely the further development of certain very important groups of wishes and to render the idea of these wishes obnoxious to the author. Ever afterwards the idea, threat, or fear of punishment was usually adequate without its actually being carried out. Most people know that a common method of correcting infants and children and preventing their persistent following of certain courses of action is by means of slaps. Most adults, however, do not realize at all that they, in their turn, have been very profoundly affected and modified all through their lives by means of the repressed effects of similar punishments received in their own infancy.

Even physical results such as the occurrence of specific diseases may occur as the ultimate effects of such early mental injuries owing to their very complicated after-results as life proceeds exerting various subtle effects upon the general metabolism of the body, rendering it far more susceptible to attack than it would otherwise be. In the author's own case he found that such after-effects had been essential factors in the causation of acute appendicitis—owing to the resulting general mental depression rendering the action of the alimentary canal far more sluggish than it would otherwise have been and also diminishing the body's powers of resistance in other ways. It is because of this that this chapter may be considered to be of great medical and scientific importance. Obviously all this is not to say, however, that acute appendicitis can be cured by mental means once it has developed. It is clear that expert treatment at the hands of a surgeon is the only safe and sensible course to follow, leaving the aforesaid mental factors to be cured afterwards by other means —if possible. "Causation" is obviously a very different matter from cure.

It is perhaps a little remarkable **that** many people should hold the belief that it is quite impossible to bring up an infant or child to be a civilized adult without giving it physical punishment and yet be able to retain the belief that they themselves remain entirely unaffected by such infantile physical punishments. This inconsistency seems very striking.

It is believed by many observers that one person out of every two possesses some neurotic symptoms. This proportion may astonish some people, but it could be greatly reduced if adults were aware of the dangers associated with punishments and were more sympathetic and understanding with children. While punishments are sometimes necessary they should not be administered without thought and consideration. Infants differ widely and their reaction to slaps and blows, of equal intensity, might well be opposite. The point is that the force of the blows, and the resulting pain, in relation to the wishes, tends to be increased by the adults associated with the infant until the final effect tends to be of the same kind. Instead of the final reaction depending upon the disposition, it would be far more true to say that the final disposition depends to a very large degree upon the amount of physical punishment and fright in relation to the instinctive wishes received by the individual in infancy. Of course it might be argued that only weak children who would not be happy in any case and who would be no good to society or themselves anyhow would be, or are, affected by these infantile blows. However, this view cannot be maintained owing to the far greater strength of adults in comparison with infants. Infants who would have grown up very happy and very useful to themselves and to society doubtless frequently have their lives comparatively ruined in the way described.

The small boy's supposed prayer (the author recently met a similar instance in actual life), "And, Lord, make me a good boy—not too good, but good 'nuff to 'scape a lickin'", may have a bearing upon this chapter. The same would apply to the following extract from Dr. J. B. Watson's article on "Behaviourism," in the 13th edition of the *Encyclopædia Britannica* (New Vol. 1, p. 347):

A social factor steps in. The father gets to the point where his own morning nap is disturbed. He yells out "Keep quiet." The child begins then to mumble to himself—a great many individuals never pass this stage, and they mumble to themselves all through life whenever they try to think. The father does not like the child's mumbling any better than his talking aloud, and so he may slap him on the lips. Finally, the parents get the child to the point where he talks silently to himself. When his lips are closed, it is nobody's business.what is going on below. Thus we come to behave as we please if we do not give any external motor sign of it—in other words, our thoughts are our own.

While agreeing with much of the above, the author may say, however, that he has no sympathy whatever with certain features of the doctrine of Behaviourism. Behaviourists nevertheless seem to have got hold of some idea of the great and, in certain respects, almost fundamental, importance of slaps in infancy which most psycho-analysts do not yet seem to have realized at all.

Everybody knows that infants are not always little angels; and, as blows or smacks of some kind have invariably to be given in infancy, the question arises as to the dose of force, and resulting physical pain, which is to be, or should be, administered—particularly with regard to seeing that the dose of pain to the infant does not exceed a certain amount, and preferably the minimum amount, required for the deterring effect. Also the question arises as to which part of the infant's body the smacks had better be applied.

With regard to these two points, the author would say that, from his experience, an important thing to avoid is blows the force of which travels longitudinally down, or along, the infant's extended arms. Blows, the force of which travels in this way, and the resulting compression waves, can certainly cause very violent pain and aching indeed to a small infant's arms, with resulting heavy repression, even if the blows are not very heavy. The author so clearly remembers this in his own case, though whether this is due to the epiphyses of the bones of the young infant being very delicate, or owing to the growing and delicate nature of the bones generally, the author does not know enough about the anatomy of the infant's arm to say. In addition to these likely factors, it is evident that, because of the small diameter of the young infant's arms, the density of shock per unit of transverse area would be much greater than in the case of an adult. It is clear that the ears and head generally should also be avoided. Probably the buttocks are the best place to receive the necessary slaps. Indeed, a friend of the author thought that they are so suitable for the purpose, being padded with flesh, that they might almost have been designed by nature specially for this purpose!

It may be considered that the results described in this chapter concerning the psychological significance of early slaps are founded upon too few instances to show that they are of general application. Naturally further work by other observers is necessary to confirm or disprove them. Of course the subject, dealing as it does with the usually completely hidden effects of repressed infantile punishments, is a very painful one to the unconscious mind and thus lends itself admirably to the production of opposing rationalizations by adults. However, the phenomena referred to were so very marked in the author's case that he can only feel that further work on the part of other people will result in their confirmation. As already mentioned, however, many of the points dealt with in this chapter can be confirmed immediately by direct observation of infants and children.

Physical punishment which does not frustrate strong primitive instinctive wishes may have little or no permanent effect upon the mind. In the same way a severe and doubtless very painful physical shock, such as must have been produced by the author's falling off (according to his parents) a chest of drawers at the age of 3, which put his shoulder out, if it has nothing to do with the intimate constitution of the personality, has no lasting psychical effect whatever. The author not only has no conscious memory of the event, but not the slightest trace of it appeared in the self-analysis. It does not seem to have exerted the slightest pathological effect upon his mind. Of course it was not frustrating any instinctive wish.

Several psycho-analysts have criticized this chapter on the ground that it makes no mention of the disappointment or frustration of love which, they consider, would be the chief cause of the harm done by infantile punishments, for they thought that all psycho-analytic experience would lead to the conclusion that this is of primary importance.

The author would be very interested to know whether by this is meant (1) frustration or cessation of love on the part of the adult to the infant caused by the infant's doing something which offends the "feelings" or opinions of the adult; or (2) frustration of possible love feelings of the infant to the adult. In his opinion it would not do to assume that the two things are inseparable,

112

or that the second follows inevitably from the first.

Undoubtedly (1) is possibly very important, for if it were not for the infant's doing something which offends any love (or protective) feelings of the adult towards it, it might be impossible for the adult to administer painful "corrective" physical punishments to the infant; but with regard to (2) the author has not found the slightest trace whatever of it in his self-analysis, and is thus unable to say anything about it.

There are clearly several possible explanations of this, such as—(a) the pain may be administered by an ill-tempered adult towards whom the infant has never had love feelings in any case, so that there were no love feelings to be frustrated, (b) in the case of an adult towards whom the infant possibly had love feelings, its mind may possess some automatic repairing mechanism which completely heals, possibly within a short time, any damage caused by this frustration so that no trace of any such effect appeared in the self-analysis, or (c) the infant under the age of 2 years, with whom this chapter is primarily concerned, may be entirely wrapped up in itself (narcissism). Naturally the author does not know if any of these explanations are correct as he has no information on the subject, not having found any trace of the matter. On the other hand, what is certain, and very important, is that the effects of physical pain, as described, remain in full in a repressed form. As a result of his researches, the author can vouch for this and its great importance. Perhaps such a possible healing process as that referred to in (b) might occur by the infant's transferring its affection to some other adult who had not ill-treated it, or to a pet animal, or even to its inanimate toys.

The author can say quite definitely that the slap given by his father at the age of 6 months did not frustrate any love feelings at all towards the latter, at that time, because he did not possess any. His father was only a "big objectionable object"—for what he did—at this age. However the slap may have been frustrating possible love feelings towards the mother. The author thinks that it simply frustrated his primitive feeling of omnipotence, along with a strong desire to feed when very hungry. Also it may have frustrated the pleasure of lying near the warmth of his mother's body. Some of these may very likely be infantile components, and prototypes, of normal adult love feelings. In this case we can well understand infantile punishments permanently damaging adult love feelings. The author is sure that the late Professor Freud was undoubtedly right in regarding an instinct as being something very completely and entirely inside the individual possessing it.

The whole of the author's results go to show that it is the permanent repression of the *instincts* of the infant by the pain of the physical punishments which is the sole important thing—whether it is the primitive feeling of omnipotence, an urgent need to feed caused by hunger, intrinsic narcissism, pride in the genitalia, or what not. In any case any love feelings towards objects in the external world would be only one of a number of instinctive wishes which are repressed in the manner described. According to the author's analysis the very young infant (and child) certainly seems to be wrapped up in itself and its wishes (narcissism); but, while the infant undoubtedly has need for the *protection* of love, he has been unable to find any psychical need for love on its part.

Since the effects of physical punishments in infancy came to the surface so prominently in the deeper stages of the author's self-analysis, it becomes important to consider why they are not more strongly in evidence in the deep stages of ordinary analysis with an analyst. If they were, it is certain that far more would have been written and published about such punishments and their effects. It seems to the author that the failure of such incidents to appear in orthodox analysis may be mainly due to strong resistance against their disclosure to the analyst.

In current psycho-analytic theory, the analyst, as is well known, always occupies the place of the parent or parental figure (loving or hostile, good or bad) in the unconscious mind of the person who is being analyzed (analysand). In the author's view this identification is not at all exclusive, but is probably with any "big strong adult" with whom the analysand was associated in infancy. When the mind of the analysand has been deeply wounded in infancy by physical chastisement, the analyst may very likely be identified in respect of such incidents with those earlier strong adults to whom disclosures are dangerous and from whom even a violent assault may again be expected. Consequently repression continues, and the infantile punishments cannot come to complete consciousness in the presence of the analyst, so that disclosure never takes place.

The physical pain of the infantile punishments, so closely coupled with the disappointment at the non-fulfilment of the infantile instinctive wishes, rapidly forms a sort of "chemical" combination which is violently and rapidly repressed right to the base of the mind. Anybody knowing the strength of the repressions and the resulting great difficulty of digging up this "chemical" compound to full consciousness, and then analyzing it back into its constituent components again would think that this was extremely interesting work, especially as it lays bare the deep-seated underlying causation of a subsequent psycho-neurotic temperament.

To conclude, the author is convinced that a number of points in this chapter are very important indeed from the point of view of human welfare and happiness, and has written this chapter in the hope that it may help to prevent small infants being knocked about too hard and cruelly, in opposition to their instinctive wishes for which they are not to blame, by strong adults with the lasting effects described. He therefore naturally hopes that his powers of exposition have been good enough for it to have this desired result. As one goes deeper in analysis it is surprising how the likelihood increases that infants tend to be "born right" on the whole. The great difficulty is to be certain of avoiding the infant's being left alone with some adult who loses his or her temper rather badly. This doubtless accounts for much of the so-called "inheritance" of neuroticism.

Chapter Eight

On the Importance of Avoiding Castration Threats Against Children

IN THE deeper stages of the analyses of adult male neurotics Professor Freud discovered to his surprise that a very large proportion of them eventually remembered threats made in their early childhood to cut off the genitalia as a punishment for, and deterrent against, early childhood exhibitionism.

The recollection of these threats was invariably accompanied by great horror and emotional disturbance, which had previously been repressed, and this repressed horror had frequently acted as a basis upon which the neurosis had subsequently been built up. In many cases it was clear that the neurosis would never have originated at all, and in other cases would not have been nearly so severe, if this repressed horror had not been present, or if the threats in question had never been made.

The severe complex associated with these childhood threats has been named, of course, the "castration-complex," and is one of Professor Freud's discoveries which excites the greatest doubt. The author at one time shared the general view. He considered the whole idea of the castration-complex to be far-fetched and improbable. First he disbelieved in the commonness of the threats, and, secondly, when they did occur, did not believe that they could possibly have such a bad and permanent mental effect as was stated.

From his own experience, the author is rather inclined to believe that much of the doubt on the part of unanalyzed adults regarding this complex may arise from the fact that the word "castration" and its meaning is normally known only to the individual many years after the threat occurs, and even then what is meant by "castration" does not accurately correspond with the actual threat. This word, and its connotation, and the actual fright itself, are thus completely separated in his mind by a long period of time and by an enormous number of memories—many of these frequently being cover-memories with strong repression attached to them. The author's scepticism was naturally much shaken by the memories dealt with in Chapter 4.

It is certain that anybody who, as an adult, has had the experience of suddenly remembering quite clearly, after long-continued analysis, castration threats being made against him as a very small child, by overpowering adults, will want to do anything he can to avoid the incidence of similar threats against other children, perhaps his own, in the future. That is the object of this chapter. Until a very deep stage in analysis is reached, the individual may have taken only an abstract theoretical interest in anything he may have heard during analysis about the castration complex and may have thought that nothing about it could possibly apply to himself, owing perhaps to what he believes to have been his very careful and guarded upbringing. Afterwards, however, it becomes a very different matter. The fright and worry following the conscious recollection are apt to be very great—possibly worse than in the worst nightmare, largely owing to the fact that both the threats and the recollections happen in waking life, and there is thus no possibility of escaping from them by waking up.

Only those who, like the author, can remember the details of a severe castration threat, and their respective attitudes towards the world before and after this threat, are in a position to realize what a fundamental change in his outlook on life a severe castration threat can produce in the individual. Before such a threat the child may have a happy outlook upon the world but after a severe castration threat the outlook may immediately become fundamentally depressed and miserable and the individual nervous.

When the fright has been worked off in analysis by the individual realizing consciously—what he had never realized consciously before—that the threat was solely a threat and one not intended to be carried out, a great improvement in his health results, and he seems to have a different view of life from what he had had previously.

Apparently the mind goes on thinking unconsciously about a castration threat, if given, until this is reached in consciousness again and removed by analysis. There is no doubt that the lives of a very large number of people have been severely damaged by these castration threats in early childhood, and that the resulting completely repressed fear is one of the chief underlying causes of nervousness and neuroticism. The matter is thus one of very great psycho-pathological importance, for we are here dealing with the deeper etiology of the neuroses. All feelings of any "unpleasantness" of the subject, or of its "impropriety", must be put aside, and we must look at the matter from the point of view of a small child, who is the person primarily (and vitally) concerned. A deeply analyzed person automatically looks at this matter (as well as many others) from the point of view of a small child.

There seems little doubt to the author that the common attitude of unreasoning scepticism concerning the castration-complex is closely related to the fact that the majority of unanalyzed people themselves possess similar repressed fears, and thus wish to disbelieve in the existence of the complex. Many books on such subjects as "The Nervous Child" make no mention whatever of the effect of such threats—an extraordinary omission in view of their very great importance. If any extremely sceptical person were thoroughly analyzed, the unfortunate probability is that he would eventually remember, to his surprise and distress, a severe threat of this nature in his childhood. It may be mentioned, for example, that great shyness of the genitalia in adult life, instead of the primitive pride in them, is highly likely to be, in practice, one of the much less serious effects in consciousness of a completely repressed castration-complex.

Careful observation and inquiries, extending over many years, in a typical English town have convinced the author that, on the average, not more than two, or at the most three, boys out of every ten escape some threat of this nature between the ages of 2 and 6 years. The widespread incidence of the threat is certainly established.

The threats are made under the following circumstances. The small boy, when he first consciously realizes the presence of the genitalia (sometimes as early as two years old), is almost invariably extremely proud of them. On account of this fact he will be inclined to exhibit them to adults and to other children. He may probably not perform this exhibition in the presence of either of the parents owing to the same fear which may have produced an earlier Oedipus complex; but he is more likely to do so in the presence of other people, particularly persons of the opposite sex such as servants.

If the exhibition were made in the presence of a man, the latter would very likely say, "You must not do that. It is considered very improper", and might smack the child if the act were repeated. Some men might make a cutting-off threat but they would probably only do so in a half-hearted way, feeling rather ashamed of themselves. Some men may see humour in making cutting-off threats in a joking way to a child, but the attitude of the mind which can see anything funny in a remark of this kind is naturally repugnant to decent minded people. Nevertheless such jesting remarks would probably not have the very bad mental effects of apparently definitely intended castration threats because they would not be taken seriously by the child.

Experience, however, shows that, in relation to this particular matter, women are in an altogether different class from men. Many women apparently have not the slightest conception of the great mental importance of the genitalia to the small boy, and experience shows that, if a small boy exposes himself in the presence of such a woman, the latter is extremely likely to say, "If you do that it will be cut off," unless she has been specially warned not to do so. Probably this idea is activated by deep-seated unconscious hostility to the male, and especially to the male organ. This hostility has been established by psycho-analysis as being very common in women. Many women have not the slightest conception of the great harm which may be done by such a threat or they would certainly adopt some other means of deterring the child from exhibitionism. As it is the castration threats will probably be increased in severity, and may be "acted", until the desired end is attained by this particular process. It is unnecessary to dilate on the terrible nature of the fright which "acted" threats cause, for even sufficiently severe verbal threats have a very bad effect.

The natural reaction of the small child is one of pride in the genitalia and in the possession of them. He thinks them a very important part of his body and that it is quite impossible and absurd that they should be cut off. Thus, when this method of suppressing the early child-hood exhibitionism is being adopted, the threats normally have to be very severe until he eventually does become convinced. Then, when the fear is once thoroughly induced, he has a mortal dread of the whole matter, which is violently and heavily repressed, and thus has a powerful unconscious detrimental effect on his mind and life ever after unless the fear is subsequently removed by analysis.

The horror which ultimately comes to the surface in psycho-analysis when severe castration threats in childhood are eventually remembered is so great that any cautious investigator would immediately wonder whether the individual might not be "transferring back" into the early castration threats unpleasant emotion attached to many incidents in his later life. Much evidence indicates, however, that the horror arises from the great mental importance of the genitalia, and is properly attached to the castration threats as such, that is originates immediately after the threats, and is not "transferred back" from later unpleasant incidents. For instance, the improvement in health which follows immediately after the working off of the fright is one of the things which indicate this.

The chief difficulty in the way of avoiding these threats is that a child while he is between the ages of 2 and 6 years may be left alone with any one of many different persons. Most of these would doubtless not make a castration threat; but out of the number there is almost certain to be one who will, unless the child's early tendency to exhibitionism has been previously checked by some other method. It is because of this that there is such a high proportion of adult males with castration complexes of various degrees of severity.

The wide occurrence of the complex is not surprising when one considers the strength of the early childhood tendency towards exhibitionism and handling of the genitalia; and the fact that, when this occurs, a cutting-off threat is apparently such a spontaneous reaction on the part of such a large number of adults.

A biological friend said to the author recently: "When one first hears of the castration-complex the idea seems to be quite impossible, but when one looks carefully into the matter, and considers the habits of small boys, one then sees, at once, that it is probably almost impossible for a small boy to escape a threat of this kind. However, I think that it is very sad if the human mind does not possess some ways and means of repairing the likely damage caused by such threats."

With regard to the last point, it would appear that the unanalyzed human mind can only attempt to repair the damage by means of covering it over; and, in the absence of analysis, the original damage apparently remains in full force. When the fright is so great as to be completely repressed in the mind it is not accessible in the ordinary way to alteration or modification.

There is something psychologically unique about the genitalia which makes it extremely detrimental to threaten castration, while a threat to cut off the nose, thumbs, or legs, for example, would do no, or very little, harm at all. Indeed, the author knows of a case in which a threat to cut out the tongue (for impertinence) was mentally actually welcomed by the child as providing a means whereby he could displace fright arising from an earlier castration threat on to the later tongue threat. The latter then acted as one of a long series of cover-memories each member of which helped to render the original extremely terrifying castration threat more completely unconscious than it would otherwise have been.

Psychological preventive medicine will probably ultimately acknowledge a great debt to the research method of analysis for having discovered the extremely common occurrence of severe castration threats in early childhood, and the great permanent mental damage which they cause. If only the incidence of these early mutilation threats could be reduced, a considerable reduction in the incidence and severity of those later disorders (both neuroses and psychoses) which have a purely mental basis might reasonably be expected to follow. A reduction in the number of cases which would be benefited by the painful, long and laborious process of analysis would be eminently satisfactory, for there will always be far more such cases than analysts to undertake the work. It is also of course infinitely more sensible and satisfactory to endeavour to prevent disorders rather than to attempt to cure them later when they have become complicated.

In view of these facts it seems desirable that medical practitioners should warn the parents of small boys of the great danger they incur in leaving them alone with unreliable people who have not been given definite instructions not to make mutilation threats against the genitalia. They should be told that, in the case of exhibitionism, the child is to be repeatedly told that this is very improper and that he must not do it; and that, if this fails, the fact is to be reported to the parents. Possibly the best method of countering the exhibition-ism is to arouse some other interest in the child's mind immediately. It is, however, unfortunately, almost impossible to be certain that these instructions would reach every person who might be left alone with the child—for example a relative or friend of a servant may be in the house. In view of this difficulty it might be advisable for the parents of a small boy to tell him, not later than the age of two, that he must not expose the genitalia in the presence of anybody. Also that if anybody ever makes a cutting-off threat against these parts, he is not to be frightened, for there is no possibility whatever of its being carried out, also that he is at once to report any such threat to the parents. If repeated prohibitions are not effective in preventing exhibitionism, punishment by moderate smacking on the buttocks, for example, might be tried.

It is so obvious that this would be an infinitely more sensible and appropriate form of deterrent. Admittedly it might give more physical pain and might not act so rapidly as the other method; but the great trouble, of course, about these inhuman castration threats during early childhood is that they penetrate so deeply into the mind, and are apt to do so very much more than is intended.

If physical pain, by moderate smacking if necessary, could be substituted for them this would certainly conduce very greatly indeed to the subsequent mental health and stability of the individual as well as to his happiness.

Chapter Nine

Psycho-Analysis and Early Complexes

THE SERIOUS psychological dangers involved in giving an infant or small child too painful slaps or blows, especially with anger or loss of temper, in order to prevent it from carrying out perfectly natural instinctive desires, have been sufficiently emphasized in Chapter 7. Such physical chastisement does much less harm after the period of early childhood, up to about the sixth year, is over. This is the period during which the foundations of a sound and cheerful personality should be laid down, and it is also the period in which seriously painful events are most subject to repression—the "amnesic" or "forgetfulness" epoch of a child's life. Of course it may be argued that people are bound to get painful shocks in life sooner or later, and the sooner they get used to them the better. But this is a wholly mistaken view which ignores the special character of the first years of a child's life. When those are past the child still has to adapt itself to the external world, and while doing so it must naturally experience various frustrations and disappointments. However these will then not cause so much harm.

Blows and frights under the circumstances indicated may gravely depress a child's mentality and render him far less happy and contented as an adult than he would otherwise have been, without any awareness that he is far less happy and contented than he might have been—owing to this depression having started during the forgetfulness period of his childhood. He cannot remember at all without analysis the comparatively very happy days of his extremely early infancy, before the blows and frights occurred, as a standard for comparison with his later relatively unhappy condition.

One of the things which impresses a person most in the deeper stages of analysis is how very helpless and weak he felt as a child in comparison with the much stronger adults around him. This condition of weakness and feeling unable to protect oneself is, of course, much more strongly emphasized at the time of receiving physical chastisement from adults than at other times. Nevertheless the feeling persists in an unconscious form after the chastisement is over. The position is an unhappy one, and it is not to be wondered at that the associated feelings are probably one of the chief causes of the forgetfulness period of childhood and of people's opposition to subsequent analysis. It is very difficult to remove in analysis the painful emotion attached to blows received in early infancy at the hand of adults: partly because of this associated emotion of helplessness which conflicts so strongly with the primitive feeling of omnipotence. Still, the emotion can all be removed eventually by continued free-associations, although it is sometimes a long process. When it is removed the basis of neuroticism is also cut away, exposing the healthy underlying strata. The object of analysis (apart from its research objects) might be described as being to return a person to the vigorous and healthy condition he was in when only a few months old.

Those physicians who attach most importance to the

current conflicts of later life are almost certainly wrong and it would appear that they can only hold this view through lack of deeper knowledge. The author wondered for a long time whether emotion might not be projected from later conflicts down into the earlier ones, in the course of analysis. Still deeper analysis makes it clear, however, that the opposite is the case.

It is the first time, as far as the author is aware, that anybody has undertaken self-analysis nearly so extensively and deeply as he has done. It is certainly very interesting, and possibly important, that the results of this work confirm Professor Freud's view that it is the complexes of infancy and early childhood which are the causes of the particular mental dispositions that render the later conflicts possible. The author has maintained a very critical attitude on this point all along because its importance is obvious. However, when the early complexes were reached and removed by analysis all traces of the later conflicts automatically disappeared. This seems strong evidence of their real causation.

Cases of mental war strain are, of course, instances of current conflicts. It is of interest that cases of "shell-shock" in the last war were found to have a previous psycho-pathological history.

The total emotion removed in analysis may not necessarily be equal to the sum of that formerly attached to each of the separate incidents dealt with, since some at least of the emotion is apparently transferred to the later incidents from the prototypes. An underlying infantile complex carrying twice the painful emotion of another may double the time required for an analysis down to its level owing to the greater amount of "free floating" repressed emotion resulting from this complex which attaches itself to each of the later incidents and which has to be worked off in relation to them before the complex itself is reached.

Certain widely held views about the mentality and reactions of children are probably quite erroneous, and in other cases only half the truth. For instance, in the chapter "The Psychology of the Child" in the small booklet *Everyday Psychology in the Nursery* (published by the "National League for Child Welfare," London), the late Dr. Charles W. Hayward says: "At birth a baby's brain resembles a photographic plate or a phonographic disc. Unconsciously, it starts from the very moment of its birth to record its environment."

The actual condition of affairs is very different. The infant's mind should, of course, not be pictured at all or in any way as a photographic plate. Instead of its being a static, merely recording, mechanism of that nature the child's mind is of course actually highly dynamic and should be regarded more as a rapidly growing young tree. When a person hits or frightens a child too severely in opposition to its instincts he does not merely put something into a lifeless photographic emulsion, but risks pushing the young tree's roots unnaturally far down into the ground, or lopping off various branches, and may very easily do permanent damage which will prevent it from ever being able to grow into a satisfactory adult tree unless the damage is removed and repaired by subsequent analysis.

Blows and slaps in infancy, associated with unfulfilled instinctive wishes as described, tend to turn large portions of the mind back upon themselves, and render it forever after unable to direct itself fully or completely on to the external world. This condition is of course known as the "introverted" type of character in the adult. On the other hand, if the young tree is not badly damaged in its early stages, when it grows into an adult tree it can shoot its branches high into the air, or spread itself into the external world, producing the "extroverted" type of character. Blows and slaps in infancy, accompanying frustration of fundamental urges so that the whole experience is repressed, are the chief cause of subsequent unconscious fears and the "inferiority feelings" in adults of which we have heard so much.

Infants, after they have received their first painful punishment at the hands of an adult, are, for ever after, apt to be inwardly suspicious and cautious of any individual who comes into the category of an adult whether he has already administered punishment to them or not. For all the child knows he may do so at any moment. As suggested, this is perhaps the chief reason why the importance of physical punishment in infancy has not come to the surface in analysis with personal analysts although it becomes so strongly apparent in the deeper stages of self-analysis. The thoughts and feelings indicated are not always fully realized in consciousness by the child at the time of their occurrence because they are so quickly repressed owing to association with the repression of the earlier punishments. Subsequent analysis however causes them to be fully realized, for it ultimately brings all these thoughts and feelings to the surface.

As is well known to psycho-analysts this attitude of unconscious suspicion on the part of children makes it extremely difficult, or almost impossible, for any unanalyzed adult to be able to understand the deeper internal workings of a child's mind. The child will not give him the required truthful information because he is unconsciously afraid to do so. Unanalyzed adults can, of course, obtain some superficial knowledge of the working of the infantile mind; but they are probably much mistaken if they think they can understand it at all well. It is very difficult even for an analyzed person to do so.

These facts remind one of some remarks by the late Dr. S. Ferenczi who was distinguished for his insight into the infantile thought processes, and who said:[1] "Indirect contradiction, which here quite unconsciously formed an obsession, evidently has its source in similar conscious reactions of small children who through their lack of courage and self-confidence are compelled to adopt this mediate speech when they want to contradict an adult. Once I said to a boy, aged 5, that he need not be afraid of a lion, for the lion would run away if only he would look him straight in the eyes. His next question was: 'And a lamb can sometimes eat up a wolf, can't it?' 'You didn't believe my story about the lion,' said I. 'No, not really—but don't be cross with me for it,' answered the little diplomatist. Analyti-

[1] See the chapter "Symptom-Constructions During Analysis," page 203 *et seq.*, "Sex in Psycho-Analysis." Badger, Boston. London Agent, Stanley Phillips.

cal experience makes it highly probable that many intelligent children, at the stage of repression marked by the latency period, before they have gone through the 'great intimidation,' regard adults as dangerous fools, to whom one cannot tell the truth without running the risk of being punished for it, and whose inconsistencies and follies have therefore to be taken into consideration. In this children are not so very wrong."

The late Mr. Havelock Ellis wished the author to write an article upon the relationship between the sexual and self-preservative instincts, kindly saying that he thought it would be valuable on account of the depth the author had penetrated into his mind and adding that he thought many psycho-analysts overestimated the importance of the sexual instinct in relation to the self-preservative one. Sir Robert Armstrong-Jones wrote to the author saying: "The first law is self-preservation with fear as its chief mechanism . . . . next comes the preservation of the race which Freud has elevated into the chief place. He stated that many mental illnesses are the result of a conflict between these two groups of instincts."

Professor Freud (p. 216 of Vol. 4 of *Collected Papers*) wrote of "the irreconcilable antagonism between the demands of the two instincts—the sexual and the egoistic." The author does not find that there is primitively any irreconcilable antagonism at all between these two instincts; but that, on the other hand, they are fundamentally very closely connected and coordinated indeed in the individual psyche.

The individual mind in infancy strives its very best

to maintain its original unity and has considerable capacity for doing so. It is only when the force and pain of the punishments from adults against the infantile sexual and other wishes become too strong that dissociation between the various instincts occurs. Then the repressed fear of the pain of the punishments remains actively at work within the mind itself to maintain this dissociation all through life in the absence of deep analysis. As already described this repressed fear tends to prevent the individual from carrying out any wishes in later life which unconsciously remind him of the earlier actions for which punishment was administered, this fear doubtless arising from the underlying self-preservative instinct. This is how the division between the two instincts, or their apparent irreconcilability to which Professor Freud referred, occurs. The antagonism is not primitive at all, as Professor Freud's remark may rather imply, and as he may perhaps have thought.

The author is thus compelled to think that it is the operation of the self-preservative instinct, acting through fear, which is the underlying cause in the production of neurosis, after pain has been experienced, since it is this unconscious and repressed fear which distorts the later sexual and other wishes and causes them to be repressed, thus preventing them from being carried out.

Investigation shows that the presence of unsatisfied sexuality—which the individual is afraid to satisfy owing to the conscious or unconscious memory of punishment, or of feared later punishment—is apparently generally an essential element in the production of the actual neurosis, and is probably usually the chief factor. Indeed, until a person had penetrated very deeply into the human psyche it might very likely appear to be the sole cause. It seems clear that many analysts have not yet penetrated so deeply into the mind as might be desired.

The author doubts the correctness of the view that Professor Freud underrated the importance of the self-preservative instinct. He dealt with what his investigations showed to be the causes of the psychoneuroses, and it is undoubtedly true that repressed components of the sexual instinct have a very great bearing indeed upon this matter in very many cases—perhaps in the majority of them. However, as far as the author is aware, Professor Freud never minimized the importance of the underlying self-preservative instinct. Although the egoistic impulses appear much earlier, in the author's experience, than the sexual, it would surely be quite useless to point this out to a patient who was badly neurotic owing to sexual repression. The patient would surely have to work through all his former repressions by the method of free-association before he could become well. An inner realization of the causes of his thoughts and behaviour coming from within the patient's own mind is apparently the only important and helpful thing from a therapeutic point of view; and, for this purpose, continued and unhindered free-association is probably the ideal method and indeed perhaps the only effective one.

Why should the young infant's undoubted great interest in itself and in its instinctive wishes—it certainly seems to love itself and its wishes—necessarily be sexual in any way although the author, as a descriptive term, has referred to it as "narcissism" or as being "narcissistic"? The author was unable to find any trace of any sexual ideas in the deeper forms of it, although looking out for them and searching carefully for anything of the kind in view of Professor Freud's theories. It seems to him, on the other hand, to be entirely egoistic in nature, which egoism later normally transforms some of its energy ("libido") into sexual impulses and into sexual love for an external object. It is these facts which cause the author to think that, while many of the components of the adult sexual impulse are certainly very deep and widespread and apparently go back into the first year of life, they may nevertheless very likely derive their energy from the still earlier egoistic feelings and impulses.

It has been said "There is no stronger love than the love for food." Why should this love be sexual at all? The author does not think it is and so far has not been able to find any evidence in favour of the other view. Because the pleasure in the mucous membranes and nervous system when eating a good meal when one is very hungry may present close analogies with some forms of sexual pleasure, it does not seem to follow from this that the former is sexual. Both forms of pleasure may very likely be fundamentally derived from the same source. In opposition to the general psycho-analytic view, he thinks that there are many different kinds of love, and that sexual love is only one of them. While having to agree that sexual components appar-

136

ently go back into the first year of life, he is thus never-theless unable to agree, owing to lack of evidence, with the late Professor Freud's very deep and widespread extension of the conception of sexuality if the matter be carried deeper than this, but considers that probably the correct view is to look at the matter the other way round—viz., the infantile components and prototypes of the adult sexual instinct, and the adult sexual instinct itself, being an extension of egoism, or of the primitive feeling of omnipotence. This view appears to be very different from that held by the late Professor Freud.

The author has reached his view quite independently through investigating the depths of his own mind. However, when one considers the development of vertebrates, it seems probable that individualistic feelings and impulses would develop earlier and be more fundamental and important than the impulses tending towards reproduction of the individual.

Even if this be so, it, of course, in no way diminishes the very great importance of Professor Freud's dis-covery of the immense part played by the repression of sexuality in the etiology of the psychoneuroses and in other directions, the underlying mechanism of which repression is dealt with elsewhere in this book.

Sublimation of the energy of instincts, or of primitive wishes and desires, is not at all the conscious process, almost under the control of the will, that one might gather from some popular writings. It arises owing to the energy behind the wishes having become repressed and locked in the deeper layers of the mind, owing to fear, so that this energy is forced to discover various in-

137

direct outlets and leakage paths into consciousness in order to obtain relief—leakage paths that will not be followed by punishment, but preferably by social credit.

The author remembers reading an essay by Arnold Bennett in which the opening sentence was: "Did you ever know an ambitious man who was happy or an unambitious man who was unhappy? I never did." It seems now possible to understand some of the mental mechanisms behind these phenomena. An ambitious man is unhappy because of the strain in the deeper layers of his mind caused by the repressed energy of instinctive wishes, energy which needs and seeks an outlet and obtains it in the pursuit of ambition. An unambitious man has not so many instinctive repressions and thus tends to be more contented and happy in any case.

It may seem a great pity that some people refuse to have children because there is neuroticism in their families, and they believe that this is inherited. While this may possibly be so in some cases, due to a specific organic basis, the author doubts its general applicability very much. It cannot be too strongly emphasized that high intelligence is certainly inherited and such highly intelligent children suffer far more mentally, and ultimately physically, from the threats and punishments of infancy than ones who are not so mentally alert. If they could be protected adequately from these they would grow up quite all right. For instance an 'acted' castration threat may be much worse for a highly intelligent child than for a duller one because the intelligent child resists the threat for a longer time since he cannot believe that it will be carried out. The threats are therefore greatly increased in severity. A point comes when the resistance breaks down, the child is really convinced that it will be carried out, and the shock becomes much more severe. It is undoubtedly true, as Professor Freud said, that many adults have no idea whatever of the extent of the cruelty they commit when they make severe castration threats against small children. It is exactly like making a similar believed threat against a fully grown individual with the added difference that the child is far more helpless and knows very well how completely helpless he is.

Castration threats, if severe, appear to make at the time of their occurrence deep wounds right through the human mind down into the more animal mind of the child, and it is very difficult to repair this deep-seated damage by the process of free-association from the level of consciousness. For a sound repair, the psychical wounds naturally have to be healed from their bases upwards instead of being merely covered over, and this takes a long time to effect thoroughly—by the mind realizing gradually as a result of extensive free-associations that the threat was solely a threat. It is not in any way true (as a friend of the author thought) that he might be very depressed until he eventually remembered the threat, but that, directly he remembered it, he would at once cheer up and become immediately well, because the matter was so absurd. It should be realized that the wounds have very probably been so severe as to modify the individual's behaviour (since this was their object), and also his reaction to life, very considerably ever since they occurred.

It seems to the author that it is, and must be, quite impossible for an individual to recover in any way completely from the effects of a severe castration threat during the latter half, or towards the end, of a twelve months' period of analysis by a personal analyst, even with the, aid of a strong positive "transference", for too few free-associations for the purpose would be produced in this time, even if the complex itself was reached at all during such a period. It takes years to remove the effects of a severe castration complex completely and even then one cannot be quite sure. Of course great good may be done by the analysis in other directions.

The author has thought for a long time that the incomplete therapeutic effects of an analysis, sometimes reported in the medical journals, very probably frequently arises from these facts. As mentioned in the Preface, the process of self-analysis described may be found very useful not only in the first place by people who have not been analyzed by a personal analyst, but also for continuing the process of analysis after leaving a personal analyst, since there is no time limit until a complete and radical cure is effected.

It should be realized that normal children are highly intelligent and might be said to be small men and women in disguise, although it would be far truer to say that adults are disguised children, so doubtless the matter should be put the other way round. The author has never been so intelligent after the slap received from his father at the age of six months as he was before it, as his recollected speed of thought before the occurrence of the slap shows. The slap produced a certain amount of repression of his pristine intelligence, because it sharply checked the natural carrying out of his desires. From this it appears clear that what educationists and industrialists are measuring by intelligence tests, which increases up to a point with advancing age, can only be intelligence with regard to external or social subjects; and cannot possibly be the fundamental or underlying intelligence of the individual with regard to such "selfish" subjects as feeding.

The repression of the emotion associated with the infantile complexes certainly sometimes eventually does a great deal of harm to the individual. It has already been mentioned that the resulting depression from their after-effects in later life can upset the digestion and, with this, the metabolism of the whole, or of specific organs, of the body. Before beginning analysis, the author suffered from a slight internal nasal inflammation for which he consulted a distinguished nose and throat specialist and mentioned to the latter that he thought of being analyzed. The specialist endeavoured to dissuade him from this intention and asked him why he thought of following this plan, to which the author replied, "Because I think there's something in it." To this he received the response, "Oh well, I'm a surgeon and I deal with facts."

Here we see the refusal to recognize mental facts to which Professor Freud often referred. It may appear from a superficial point of view that this opposition may be founded upon the crude scientific materialism of the nineteenth century which regarded mental facts, even though they are facts, to be *imponderabilia* and unworthy of careful and critical scientific study and investigation. It would doubtless be far more correct to say, however, that the crude scientific materialism of the nineteenth century and later was, and is, on the other hand, itself probably founded upon and produced by a wish or desire not to investigate mental facts owing to the presence of complexes in the minds of the people concerned.

As his analysis proceeded, the author found that the nasal trouble had only been able to infect him owing to slightly lowered health caused by mental depression produced by certain unhappy events in his life, for when the depression produced by these events was removed from his mind the inflammation completely disappeared. Even before analysis the author was faintly aware that the trouble had only started after the depressing events in question. The dealing with these "mental facts" themselves by free-association produced a far more complete removal of the inflammation than the special vaccine which the specialist prepared.

In this connection the following extract from a report of the London Zoo may be of interest: "Probably the majority of wild animals harbour intestinal parasites which seem to do them little harm while they are in normal health. But change of diet or of surroundings, and especially moping, often lower the state of health and give the opportunity for a rapid multiplication of the parasites, which may then prove dangerous to the hosts themselves."

Some people think that the analyst reads the reported thoughts into the mind of his patient. This is not so, however, provided the process is properly conducted and the analyst confines himself to asking the patient what he is thinking about and inquiring the connection between the free-associations produced at different times. The opposition to the recognition and careful scientific investigation of mental facts is interesting. If, for example, a person tells an analyst he is thinking about subject A and then that he is thinking about subject B, and if it is later on found that both these thoughts depended upon subject C, which he recollected later, and which was previously repressed in his mind, the analyst can carefully observe and record these various facts, which are objective and external to the analyst, as carefully as he might observe and record various objective facts which he might meet in any ordinary branch of natural science. Analysis when properly carried out consists, as described, of a careful objective study or investigation of a person's mind right down to early infancy.

Of course many people think that it is impossible to make such a careful objective study of the mind—owing to what they term its creative and imaginative faculty, which causes it to produce imaginary structures such as phantasies and day-dreams which, they consider, would lead the investigator astray. Professor Freud, however, believed that no imaginary structure of this kind could be produced without some previous basis of fact or experience to found it upon; and investigation certainly seems to support his view.

Indeed, when one looks carefully into the matter it seems to be only common sense. The late Sir Frederick

Mott pointed out to the author that he could not see how it could be otherwise and that it seemed clear to him that every phantasy and dream must necessarily contain some fact or experience derived from the external world, and that it seemed obvious that no phantasy or dream could possibly be formed by the brain without this information. Professor Tansley wrote to the author: "Fantasies are always compounded from actual experiences acting upon the mentality of the individual concerned. Every psychical 'presentation' is and must be the joint product of external and internal factors. No fantasy could possibly be constructed without some experience. This fact is far too often forgotten and lost sight of or never realized."

The repression of the surprise and humiliation caused by his, to him, unexpected defeat by his father referred to in Chapter 6, constituted, when repressed, the only part of the Oedipus complex which the author has been able to find in his case. Still the surprise and mental feelings produced by his first defeat were so great that this form of the complex could, in his case, only be described as being fairly strong. It will, however, be seen that his Oedipus complex was apparently only associated with egoistic and nutritive feelings and not at all with any sexual ones. It might possibly have eventually run on these other lines if it had been able to take a free course; but the unconscious memory of this early defeat certainly prevented any such developments from becoming specific. This is not to say that this complex may not frequently be sexual, and it may have had repressed unconscious components of this nature, repressed by this early defeat, in the author's case.

The author considers after long experience that it is impossible for anyone to controvert at all effectively the results of careful and long continued analysis—either the truth of the early memories recalled by it or its ultimate therapeutic effect. The unfortunate thing is, however, that the rapid and complete repression of the fear and pain associated with the forgetting of the important infantile complexes, and the resulting comparatively depressed attitude, frequently acts as a basis for the subsequent creation of far more serious pathological structures than a mere disbelief in the results of analysis.

After his experience, the author is somewhat amused by people who utter very strong views against psychoanalysis and even go to the extent of writing articles against it—without troubling to look into the matter at all carefully and without applying the "acid test" of trying the process on themselves—or having it tried on themselves—even for a short period. In the case of open-minded people this is probably chiefly because they do not know the proper method of working, and indeed the method of free-association does take some considerable time to get accustomed to properly. In regard to other people who think it "a most unhealthy subject," this is probably a projection of their own minds and means that their minds are in a very unhealthy condition with many repressions and much worry which they would rather not think about bearing down upon them. Many people's minds seem unfortunately to be in this condition.

145   L

Such people intuitively realize that the analytic process would bring this worry to the surface and thus they are strongly prejudiced against the whole subject. They do not realize, however, that this worry is continually depressing them even when it is repressed and that analysis only brings as much trouble to the surface as the mind can stand at any given moment—owing to the activity of the so-called "censorship". This particular little bit of worry is then gradually removed by further free-associations indicating the best way out of it; and, in this way, all the worry and causes of worry are gradually removed from the mind.

It is clearly not fair to blame analysis for worry pre-existing in the mind perhaps before analysis was ever heard of, and which it had no part whatever in causing, but which, on the other hand, it might be able to remove. Psycho-analysis is thus, in the author's opinion, an extremely healthy subject with a very beneficial motive and effect when properly handled. Some of its essential features were suggested by Dr. Breuer's famous patient and the process was developed by Professor Freud because it was found to be very beneficial to neurotic people. Its value will probably in the long run chiefly be as a research method for discovering the causes which later produce those disorders that have a purely mental basis and so enable preventive medicine to reduce the incidence of these disorders in the future. It is obviously so much more sensible, practical and economical, to prevent a disorder from ever occurring than to attempt to cure it when it has developed—no matter how remarkable the cure may be. The author considers that psycho-analysis as a research method for investigating the causation of mental disorders is invaluable; and that opposition to its employment for this purpose on blind and prejudiced grounds is probably only objecting to the inevitable. It must be remembered that most independent and critical workers who have investigated the mind in an unbiased way by the process of free-association have reached results in some respects very similar to those of Professor Freud and have confirmed various discoveries of his. This has happened so often that it can hardly be chance.

As far as the author's experience goes, it seems to him that an undue amount of attention is given in some analytical literature to "anal-erotism" and to a few other tendencies in comparison with the importance of the infantile complexes. While the author is prepared to believe in the great importance—from the point of view of subsequently having a happy life—of adequate and regular satisfaction of so-called "oral-erotism" during the first year of life, he has been only able to find very slight traces, or none at all, of any so-called "anal-erotism." "Oral-erotism" he would also personally prefer to describe as simply "hunger" as this seems to him to be by far its most important component even if there should be others.

Many psycho-analysts have very strong opinions in favour of the view that the "repressed" mental material, after it has been repressed into the unconscious, should still be regarded as mental and not, for example, physiological. The author thinks that they are certainly right, for he does not see how the facts of symbolism and of dream formation can be explained in any other way. On the view that the repressed material is "physiological" when it is brought to the surface of consciousness it again becomes "mental," and we cannot understand such jumps from psychical to physiological and back again. Hence the psycho-analytic view that the whole set of processes must be conceived of as being mental though part is repressed and unconscious. The repressed mental material, while it is repressed, undoubtedly has in any case very important physiological effects—a fact which many opponents of analysis would not like to admit.

Kant with his "categorical imperative" admitted that he knew nothing about the conscience but regarded it as the final voice. Analysis, however, tells us a great deal about the origin of the conscience, and the way in which it develops. In this respect, as well as in many others, analysis is far more penetrating than philosophy. Freud's work showed, as has been well said, that "man is not a rational but a rationalizing animal", and most philosophy consists of rationalizing. It may be mentioned, for example, that the infantile complexes severely modify the philosophical attitude of a person. In particular they tend to turn his philosophy away from a feared reality on to the more idealistic, theoretical, and abstract, aspects of phenomena.

Malinowski, from his studies of certain Melanesians of the Trobriand archipelago, found that amongst the Trobrianders proper, where there is comparatively little repression from infancy onwards he could not find a single adult man or woman who was hysterical

148

or even neurasthenic. Nervous tics, compulsory actions or obsessive ideas were not to be found. In the neighbouring islands of the Amphletts, however, peopled by a similar race, but where the infantile and other repressions were much stronger, his first and strongest impression was that this was a community of neurasthenics. As Malinowski pointed out, it would appear that a detailed investigation of these two neighbouring communities would afford a brilliant objective confirmation of psycho-analytic discoveries.

Chapter Ten

Additional Notes

THE REPRESSED fear of dying in the workhouse mentioned in the second paragraph on p. 24 was caused by the author's mother having been a Guardian of the Poor, and thus to his having seen, as a child, on occasional visits to the workhouse, numbers of elderly persons, who seemed to him very old and very near to death.

It was doubtless not at all because of his patient's repetitions that the second analyst was "snappish" as detailed on p. 21. He did not mind repetition at all in itself but said that it interested him very much, for he always wondered what was at the back of it, and causing it, in the patient's mind. He doubtless "snapped" solely because he wanted to get the author on to some entirely different subject, thinking that this would expedite the analysis. However, the effect of this "snappishness" upon the patient's mind strongly indicates that some forms of the so-called "active" technique of analysis may retard the process instead of helping it. An inner realization of the causes of his thoughts and behaviour coming from inside the patient's own mind is apparently the only permanently beneficial thing from a therapeutic point of view.

The author's experience suggests that continued free-association on the part of the patient brings this about by itself and that it is quite unnecessary for the free-association to be supplemented by psycho-analytical interpretation of the material.

There need be no fear of a person's turning himself into a neurotic by writing down his free-associations, for the author found, as stated, that this has quite the opposite effect and removes neurotic effects from the mind. Excessive conscious "introspection", on the other hand, may very likely accentuate a tendency to neuroticism.

There appears to be a great deal of popular misconception regarding the process of psycho-analysis and of the manner in which it achieves its therapeutic results. For instance, a person does not go to a psychoanalyst at all in order to be "told" anything about his infancy or early childhood. Such "telling" would probably have comparatively little curative effect, or none at all. The therapeutic effect apparently arises solely owing to the realization of various thoughts and reactions, and the removal or "evaporation" of the emotion which was buried with them and had been hitherto unrecognized.

While the author has had little or no personal experience of transference and of its alleged usefulness as an emotional solvent, he can only feel that it is quite unnecessary for deep analysis. For this, and for the best therapeutic effect as well, it seems to him that unhindered and long continued free-association is the only beneficial and helpful thing. He is inclined to think that the effects of the transference may very likely be more an appearance and a temporary illusion than that they should have any very permanent and deep-seated curative effect comparable at all with that of long-continued free-association.

As mentioned, the pain and fear caused by the infantile punishments naturally conflicts very strongly with the primitive feeling of omnipotence. The latter appears to flow over the pain as quickly as it can so as completely to envelop and conceal it, and the foiled wishes, in a sort of closed compartment. Thus a manifestation of the primitive feeling of omnipotence has to be penetrated before this combination can be investigated by analysis, and this particular manifestation of the primitive feeling of omnipotence is apparently what is termed the "censorship".

Some people apparently think that psychology deals with "trivialities". It is difficult to see how they can hold this view for a moment in view of the number of persons inside institutions for the insane, the number of suicides, and the like.

Other people have said that psycho-analysis causes them to wonder how there can be any sane people in the world. It seems that the answer can be given quite definitely: "owing to the natural innate stability of the normal human psyche." It takes a great deal to upset it, but unfortunately this "great deal" frequently occurs.

A reader said that, while finding much food for thought in this book, and appreciating that much of what we suffer is very likely due to what we have experienced in our infancy and childhood, he nevertheless thought that it rather omitted an important qualification—why is a race horse more sensitive than a farm horse? Why is it that abnormality is far more prevalent in the upper classes than in the lower classes where rough treatment and slaps are more usual?

It seems that a race horse is undoubtedly more sensitive than a farm horse because its inherited constitution is that way and naturally sensitive things suffer more from a given amount of ill-treatment than do less sensitive ones. This greater amount of sensitiveness in the upper classes, doubtless renders them on the whole, more liable to develop abnormalities as a result of ill-treatment. With regard to the point that rough treatment and slaps are commoner in the lower classes, it is pointed out in chapter 7 that it is not rough treatment or slaps in themselves which do the permanent harm: to do this they have to be repressing some important instinct. The repression of the manifestations of the sexual instinct, for instance, is not nearly so severe in the lower classes as in the upper ones, as Freud pointed out repeatedly.

REFERENCES TO USEFUL LITERATURE

THE AUTHOR has read a large number of books upon psycho-analysis, and it may be useful to give a list of some which he has personally found most useful and interesting, although it is not suggested that there is not a large number of other useful books on the subject.

However, the author is sure that psycho-analysis cannot be learned at all by mere reading—doubtless no more than comparative anatomy or surgery can be. Reading is in no sense the equivalent of practical work in the subject, and in no way the same thing as even a superficial analysis. Actual analysis is the only method by which the importance of Professor Freud's discoveries can be brought home to the individual mind.

Practical work is, of course, of vital fundamental importance in all science, as all scientific research and enquiry is naturally founded upon it, since it is by means of practical work that we obtain the observational data upon which any book that has any claim to be called scientific is founded.

In reading such books as the following, however, one will frequently find that various passages in them tend to arouse various trains of thought and infantile memories in the mind. These matters can then be worked through, and the emotion removed from them, by means of the process of self-analysis described in this book. The author thus hopes that it will be found very useful for practical work in conjunction with the reading of other books.

"Introductory Lectures on Psycho-Analysis." By Prof. Sigmund Freud. (George Allen & Unwin, Ltd., London.) 16s.

Dr. Ernest Jones says in the Preface: "In the future we can unhesitatingly deal with the question so often asked and say: 'This is the book with which to begin a study of psycho-analysis.' "

The style in which this book is written is very pleasant and fascinating and the late Professor Freud's intellectual honesty is very apparent. The first part contains an interesting condensed account of "Psychopathology of Everyday Life" (T. Fisher Unwin, 12s. 6d.) and the second part summarizes portions of "The Interpretation of Dreams" (George Allen & Unwin, 16s.). The third part consists of a large number of later results and miscellaneous matters. "Introductory Lectures" thus resembles three books in one and is extremely good value.

"The New Psychology and its Relation to Life." By A. G. Tansley, M.A., F.R.S. (George Allen & Unwin, Ltd., London.) 10s. 6d.

This book, by the author's former Director of Studies at Cambridge, is extremely suitable for arousing interest in this new subject on account of the very interesting style in which it is written and the nature of the material dealt with.

"A General Selection from the Works of Sigmund Freud." By John Rickman, M.D. (The Hogarth Press.) 5s.

A condensed but coherent and comprehensive exposition of psycho-analysis in Freud's own words. Very readable and extremely useful.

155

"Psycho-Analysis." By R. H. Hingley. (Methuen & Co., Ltd., London.) 6s.

This book may be found useful as an introduction to more technical works. .

"Fundamental Conceptions of Psycho-Analysis." By A. A. Brill, M.D. (George Allen & Unwin, Ltd.) 12s. 6d. net.

A very interesting book written in an easy style by an authority on the subject and may be useful to those who find Professor Freud's own books somewhat advanced. It indicates many of the wide applications of psycho-analytic discoveries.

"Essays in Applied Psycho-Analysis." By Ernest Jones, M.D. (The Hogarth Press, 52 Tavistock Square, W.C.1.) 18s.

This consists of thirteen collected papers. The author's patience and industry in collecting references to literature from many parts of the world is very apparent.

"Collected Papers on Psycho-Analysis." By Ernest Jones, M.D. (Baillière Tindall & Cox, London.) 30s.

This book consists of an interesting and useful collection of about 40 papers on the subject.

"Freud's Collected Papers on Psycho-Analysis." In 4 volumes. (The Hogarth Press, 52 Tavistock Square, London, W.C.1.)

Vol. I. "Early Papers and History of Psycho-Analytical Movement." 364 pp. 21s.

Vol. II. "Clinical Papers. Papers on Instinct and the Unconscious." 416 pp. 21s.

Vol. III. "Five Case Histories." 624 pp. 30s.

Vol. IV. "Metapsychology-Dreams." 472 pp. 21*s*.

These four volumes contain all the most important of Professor Freud's original contributions and should certainly be read by anybody who desires to make a serious study of the subject.

"FURTHER CONTRIBUTIONS TO THE THEORY AND TECHNIQUE OF PSYCHO-ANALYSIS." By Dr. Sandor Ferenczi. (The Hogarth Press, 52 Tavistock Square, London, W.C.1.) 28*s*.

A very instructive collection of over 70 long and short papers on the subject by one who has contributed a very large number of original results to it.

"SELECTED PAPERS ON PSYCHO-ANALYSIS." By Karl Abraham, M.D. (The Hogarth Press, 52 Tavistock Square, W.C.1.) 30*s*.

A very useful and valuable book by one of the pioneers of the subject. It should especially interest psychologists and educationists.

"THE INTERNATIONAL JOURNAL OF PSYCHO-ANALYSIS."

Certain back volumes are obtainable—Price 30*s*. each unbound, or 40*s*. bound from the publishers, Messrs. Baillière, Tindall & Cox, Henrietta Street, London, W.C.

Besides numerous original articles this journal contains numerous book reviews and abstracts of papers. On account of this valuable information concerning further reading, any serious student of psycho-analysis would be well advised to obtain or consult the back volumes.